EXCEPTION
TO
THE RULE

BOBBY TRUFANT

Library of Congress Control Number 2009903395
Copyright © 2005 Bobby Trufant.
Published by Mullins Publications, LLC
Printed in the United States of America.
ISBN: 0-9760160-1-X
ISBN13: 9780976016014
To order additional copies visit www.amazon.com
or call 1-866-308-6235.

Cover designed by: Jamil Jones of Jay Kay Photography & Media
www.jaykayphotography.com
Vivianna's hat designed by: Yvonne LaFleur
www.yvonnelafleur.com

Dedicated to the loving memory
of
Robert & Clementine Trufant

Acknowledgements:

To my loving wife, Tia Trufant,
who shares my dreams.

Cover models:

Acy D. Brown - Bobby
Jaqueline C. Fleming - Vivianna
Devin M. Samuel - Kwamina
Xane G. Hunter - Hakeem
Anya K. Trufant - Sula

CHAPTER 1

Family Matters

It is a cool autumn afternoon with joggers, volley-ball players, and picnickers enjoying the day. Trees beginning to change colors drape Central Park. Birds are chirping and leaves are falling in the invigorating breeze, as the enticing aroma of food from street vendors saturate the air. One can clearly see the New York skyline in the background.

Onlookers watch as Bobby, a forty-one-year-old, handsome, statuesque, broad shouldered black man, tosses a perfect spiral to Kwamina, his twelve-year-old mirror image son. This pass exhibits his athletic prowess, reminiscent of his high school days. Bobby's thirty-five-year-old beautiful wife, Vivianna, whose skin tone and hair is indigenous to New Orleans seventh ward Creoles, sits on a park bench enjoying her favorite past time, reading. Hakeem, their six-year-old son, who is clearly a mixture of both his parents, mischievously throws sticks at squirrels, while their three-year-old daughter, Sula, who is the spitting image of her mother, reaches eagerly from her stroller toward the pigeons feeding nearby.

Bobby claps his hands together loudly and exclaims, "Good catch, good catch, just like I taught you!"

Kwamina throws the ball back.

"Now I want you to go long on this one. Let's see how quick you can get out there." The pass goes near a stand of trees where an older boy with tattered clothing, apparently alone, enviously looks on.

Kwamina, who is grinning from ear to ear, throws the ball back and shouts, "Head's up!" After he catches the next pass, Kwamina approaches the boy, who has a melancholy expression on his face. "Hey, what's up? My name is Kwamina."

"I'm Jeremiah, but they call me J for short. But I'm good for sure."

"Good at what?"

"Good at that," nodding towards the football.

Kwamina asks, "Hey, wanna catch a few passes?"

"Sure, you don't think that man will mind do ya? I just saw his last pass and boy he's good!"

"That's my dad. He won't mind. He was All State QB in his day. Let's go and ask him. I'll race ya."

"Man, are you sure?"

"He's cool, come on." The two boys sprint toward Bobby. When he sees them coming, he braces himself for the two charging boys. Kwamina and Jeremiah bump into Bobby; all three hit the ground laughing.

Kwamina stands up with his hands on his knees, laboring to catch his breath. "Dad, this is my new friend J. I told him you wouldn't mind if he joined us," he says, laughing. "I also told him you were cool."

Bobby horses around while tickling Kwamina. Chuckling, Bobby says, "I am cool. I am cool, right?"

Laughing, Kwamina replies, "Yeah Dad, yeah; you're the coolest."

Bobby palms Kwamina's head, pushing him backwards to the ground, while shaking his finger. "And don't you forget it!" He extends a welcoming hand to Jeremiah. "Alright J, you can play with us as long as you remember what Kwamina just said. I'm the coolest dad!"

"Deal, cool daddy!" J answers.

Exercising his authority, Bobby says, "Hey, it's Mr. Bobby. Now, you guys check this out," as he points long. "Let's see what you can do."

Kwamina and Jeremiah dash out for the pass. Kwamina catches the ball and Jeremiah runs back.

"Mr. Bobby, can I throw this one?"

"Sure, why not? I'll tell you what. This is it. I'm gonna be the defensive back and Kwamina's gonna to be your tight end. You guys huddle and we'll see if I can defend this pass, okay?"

They agree; Kwamina and Jeremiah huddle, and then come out.

Jeremiah calls out in cadence, "Hut 1, hut 2, hut, hut, hut."

Kwamina goes long; Bobby slows to a stop, thinking that Kwamina is out of range of Jeremiah's young arm. Jeremiah throws the ball and Kwamina catches it.

Bobby mentally measures the distance between Kwamina and Jeremiah, shouting, "Whoa!" He nods his head while beckoning to Jeremiah and Kwamina, "Come here." Upon Jeremiah's arrival, he sings his praises, "Young man that was a beautiful pass! I mean awesome! You've got an impressive arm kid. Where's your dad?"

"Well, I don't know where my dad is."

"Is he at home?"

"Nah," Jeremiah says, looking down sadly, "I don't have a dad."

"Man, I tell you—does your mother ever mention the name Doug Williams around the house?"

"Doug Williams? I don't think so."

Bobby laughs, "Oh no, I was just kidding! Okay, I'll tell you what. We'd better be getting along, but this is going to be the last play of the game. This is for the championship...think big! This is for the Super Bowl title and we're gonna bring it home for the Giants. It's fourth quarter...two seconds left on the clock with no time outs. That would give us time for one more play, so it's got to be the hail Mary. So you guys line up on the same side and kite out. I'll put it up for one of you to come down with it. But remember, you guys are on the same team."

Kwamina and Jeremiah run the pattern. Bobby throws the ball up. Jeremiah tries to make the catch but tips the ball up in the air. Kwamina makes the catch. Kwamina and Jeremiah celebrate with a high five and a spike, dancing in the end zone. Vivianna rises from her seat, noticing the celebration.

Jumping up running toward them, Bobby excitedly exclaims, "Yes, yes! That's what I'm talking about. I'll tell you guys, we've got something special going on here. With your arm and Kwamina's hands, we're gonna work with this. You two can easily be the next Phil Sims and Bobby Ingram."

Jeremiah is obviously moved by the statement. When Kwamina hugs his dad around the waist, Jeremiah surprises Bobby by hugging him from the other side. With a look that only a proud father would understand, Bobby hugs Jeremiah around the neck.

Kwamina walks toward his mother and introduces her to Jeremiah, "J...Mom; Mom...J."

Vivianna smiles.

"Hello ma'am."

Kwamina asks, "Dad, can J come home with us?"

"Well, no, Son, we just can't take J home like he's a stray pet. He's got his own family."

Jeremiah interjects, "No...no I don't!"

Bobby ignores the comment and offers, "He's welcome to visit any time."

Jeremiah grins from ear to ear.

"Great Dad, cause I'm tired of Hakeem. I need someone to relate to. Know what I mean?"

"Hey, don't be so quick to throw your little brother away. You may need him one day."

Kwamina sucks his teeth with disgust, "Yeah, right."

Hakeem shakes his finger at Kwamina.

Vivianna writes their phone number down and hands it to Jeremiah. "Here J."

Jeremiah accepts the paper and stuffs it in his pocket. "Thank you ma'am. I'll call you tonight Man."

"Cool! Dad, can J attend your CPR class at the firehouse tomorrow?"

"Sure."

"J, you know the firehouse on 3rd and East 102nd?"

"Yeah, I know."

"Bro, it's a cool class. You'll love it."

Bobby instructs Jeremiah, "Meet me there tomorrow."

"Uh, Mr. Bobby,…is it okay if I get there a little early?"

"Okay Son. I'll give you the nickel tour of the firehouse. You got a nickel?"

Jeremiah pats his pockets.

"Dad!"

"Okay, tomorrow on the house."

Jeremiah gives Kwamina dap and does a cartwheel and a back flip. Looking back at Bobby and Kwamina, Jeremiah exclaims, "I'll be there tomorrow…early! Yes!" with his fists clenched at waist level in a backwards motion.

Bobby and Kwamina look at each other, shrug their shoulders, and smile. Bobby replies, "I think that's one happy kid."

The family leisurely walks through the park toward the family vehicle parked in the distance. Bobby smiles, pats his chest, takes a deep breath, and sighs, "Thank you Mother Nature. No…thank you, Mother Earth, for all this fresh air."

Hakeem asks inquisitively, "Mother Earth? Dad, what you talking about?"

Kwamina raises his hand and excitedly says, "Oh…oh…Dad—"

Bobby says, "I got this. Who is Mother Nature? Who is Mother Earth?" He looks around and explains, "Well, she's the one who has given us all of this Son. She is the womb of all life and this is nature's schoolhouse."

"That's not what they say in Sunday school."

"It's what we call symbolism Son. God created all of this, of course. Try to think of Mother Nature as a sort of guardian angel—an angel who takes care of what God has created."

Hakeem, feeling left out, adds, "Like a gardener with a giant green thumb."

Bobby smiles, "Something like that. Best named by the Native Americans for their visions into the spirit world—things pertaining to nature, this entire planet—very, very deep people...people we should listen to and learn from."

Kwamina says, "The only thing I've ever seen Indians do was attack white people on wagon trains."

"Yeah, that's Hollywood for ya. Always making the underdog look like the bad guy. Native Americans lived off the land Son. They have a profound respect for all that she yields and all her creatures. They weren't the ones who needlessly slaughtered herds of buffalo."

Hakeem states, "Yeah, I saw a buffalo at the zoo one time. He was big and hairy and smelly."

"Furry, Son,...buffalos are furry, not hairy. But I digress—back to what I was saying."

Inquisitively, Kwamina asks, "Digress?"

"D-I-G-R-E-S-S. Look it up. Well, anyway, ah...for example, we live and we die, but we all have a purpose. Take that tree for instance. It lives, it gives shade, and provides a home for the birds, squirrels, and insects; then it dies. The compost nourishes the earth to provide for new growth."

Vivianna adds, "The air, the water, the sun—her elements are all we need to survive. All that is life comes from Mother Earth and sustains life." After she makes her comment, she cuts her eyes at Bobby in disgust.

Bobby instructs, "Pick up that litter kids. Let's not insult Mother Earth."

Hakeem takes cue from Kwamina and starts picking up litter and putting it in trashcans. Sula assists by pointing to some litter. The beautiful New York skyline is in view. Bobby stops and looks around.

"It's a damn shame."

Vivianna asks anxiously, hoping he remembered their anniversary, "What?"

"It's a shame that not one of those skyscrapers is owned by a black enterprise and no major black bank exists to make this dream a reality. Our only involvement Viv, is cleaning them at night and security maybe. And even more farfetched, maybe some engineers. The only thing remotely close to that reality is the Charles Avery Vincent building on 125th."

Vivianna shakes her head in agreement, dismissing her animosity towards Bobby for a moment. "You know, we're just beginning to see some real color on Wall Street."

"Yes!"

Vivianna is taken aback by his overzealous reply.

Kwamina approaches his parents and inquires, "And the Statue of Liberty?"

Vivianna sarcastically answers, "And to think, the original Lady Liberty was that of a black woman with broken chains at her feet and in her left hand. The idea was to honor the blacks who played a pivotal role in ending the Civil war, thereby abolishing slavery. But, she never made it to the harbor because it would have embarrassed the beaten south."

Bobby mockingly states, "Give me your tired, your poor, your huddled masses. Yeah right. And Ellis Island…boy did they come, but not the way we came."

Kwamina inquires, "How did we get here, Dad?"

"Mom, I know you can handle this one."

Vivianna cuts her eyes at Bobby again. "We arrived here on slave ships Son. We were dehumanized and stacked in the holes of slave ships like animals. It was a time called the Middle Passage."

Bobby pauses and looks skyward in deep reflection. "You know Viv," pausing for a moment, "sometimes I swear I can hear the moans and wails of those miserable human beings."

"I know what you mean. I can hear it too." In deep thought, she addresses Kwamina, "It happened around 1517. People were taken from their villages in West Africa. The crossing took anywhere from five to twelve weeks. Fifteen to twenty percent of the people didn't live to become slaves—the lucky ones. The conditions were deplorable…no, horrific. That sadistic diabolical captain. What's his name?" Vivianna looks at Bobby who shrugs. "Ah," closing her eyes, she found the name, "Luke Collenwood. He didn't help matters any, hence the first serving from the melting pot."

Kwamina asks, "Mom, what's this melting pot you speak of?"

"I'll explain later, Son."

Bobby pleads, "Boyee, don't get your mother started again. She's so Afro centric—that's why she named you Kwamina."

"Yes. It's a beautiful Nigerian name. It means happiness and all that is good!"

Kwamina asks, "Mama, what's Afro centric?"

"An Afro centric, Son, describes black people with a high level of consciousness or awareness relative to who they are, where they came from, and where they are going in this world as black people."

Hakeem proudly says, "I'm not Afro centric; I'm Catholic."

Sula says, "I wanna be like you, Mama—Afrolic."

Vivianna laughs, "Okay, Sula, you can be an Afro-Catholic."

Hakeem stares at a woman who is jogging. The jogger stops to tie her shoelace. Hakeem is paying close attention to her legs and cleavage. Sula notices birds feeding and flying overhead. Sula shows an interest in animals while Hakeem is exploring his budding libido.

Bobby says matter of factly, "Funny how white politicians are always talking about a level playing field. I sure ain't seen it yet."

Vivianna asks sarcastically, "Haven't seen it yet?"

"No Viv, something this serious, something that affects our lives, our kid's lives, and the lives of everyone we know. No, I ain't seen it yet. I ain't seen nothing that even resembles a level playing field. Affirmative action…that was the only way. Affirmative action was getting into some of those corporate offices downtown and now they're trying to take that back."

Kwamina wonders, "Affirmative action…what's that?"

"The best way I can explain it, Son, is to use a metaphor. Hey, remember J, our new friend?"

"Yeah Dad."

"Well, remember how he wanted to get into the game, but didn't until he felt welcome by you?"

"Yeah."

"Then once he did, we discovered just how talented J was. You see, regardless of race, we gave him the opportunity to prove himself. Now, do you understand son?"

"I think so, Dad."

Bobby gives Kwamina a reassuring hug. Kwamina looks toward his mother and siblings. "Dad, why do you hug and kiss us so much?"

"Son, it's just an expression of my love for my family. But, I'd like you to read God's definition of love, for God is love. By the way, his proper name is Yahweh or Jehovah; God is His title. Refer to your Bible tonight. Uh...the book of first Corinthians, chapter thirteen. Read verses four through eight and we'll discuss it in detail later. But, Son, I'll attempt in my own words to tell you what love means to me. It has certain characteristics...the feeling of love—expressing that feeling and sharing that feeling with your fellow man. I'll start from the beginning with this family. Bobby and Vivianna...your mom's beautiful smile attracted me to her. I didn't realize I was gawking at her. She noticed and said something I believed to be English, but it sounded like this, 'Boyeee don't you be lookin' at me like dat, no.' Son, this was my first encounter with pure New Orleans dialect and a beautiful Creole woman." He looks at Vivianna, "Do you remember the exact location?"

"Bobby, if you don't remember, I'm sure not going to tell you." She cuts her eyes and mumbles, "Can't remember anything." She is growing more disgusted by the fact that Bobby has yet to mention their anniversary, which is tomorrow. Bobby is relishing in her dismay because he is setting her up.

Bobby finishes his story, "Son, we were at Xavier University New Orleans, nineteen and seventy-five. I knew her from that cute little hat she wore all the time, rain or shine. That was her hallmark and I was attracted to that about her also. You know your mom loves her hats." He looks at Vivianna with a funny, playful face. "I remember when we were in the library. There was just something about her. I just had to get to know her better. I noticed her around campus, but when I took the time to really look at her in that library, your mom was the single most beautiful woman I'd ever seen."

Enraptured, Kwamina says, "Oooh Mom."

Vivianna smiles broadly, waves in acknowledgement, and goes back to reading.

"Yes, and she was doing what she loves to do most—read! We became best friends and I knew I was in love when she took me home and gave me a piece of grandmere's sweet potato pie! Oooh, Son, the food down there! Between the Cajuns, Creoles, and many other cultures that settled in Louisiana with their spices and recipes, their food is the best in the world."

Kwamina adds, "Oh yeah, I sure miss grandmere's sweet potato pie."

Bobby gives Kwamina ¬dap. "I know that's right. We're going to have to call grandmere real soon. Now you've got me digressing again! Back to your mom. If it wasn't love at first sight, it was something I can't put my fingers on. In fact, she wouldn't let me put my fingers on anything! Boy, I tell you, your mama was something else; but she was ALWAYS a lady. Grandmere and grandpere raised your mama right."

Kwamina looks back and forth from his mom to his dad.

Vivianna says, "Don't worry about it; leave that alone."

Shaking his head, Bobby smiles broadly and chuckles, "Then she moved in for the kill with the big guns. She cooked for me what you like."

"Gumbooooo!"

Sula adds, "Oh, Mama, I love when you cook dat jumbo and gumbolia."

Excited and feeling left out, Hakeem says, "I like grandmere's red beans. Mama, can you cook us some red beans and rice?"

"Sure, but you know what red beans do to you boy."

Kwamina changes the subject, "Dad, was mom as beautiful then as she is now?"

"Sure she was Kwam. She was just so cute."

Vivianna's reaction is one of quiet pleasure.

"A couple of dress sizes smaller maybe, and she always had on that little hat. She was as cute as a little spotted pup pulling a red wagon."

Kwamina looks at his dad smiling.

"Hey, it's something I heard down south and I have no idea just how cute that is!" When Bobby attempts to kiss his wife, she shuns him. "Son, there is an old saying—beauty is only skin deep. Don't get hung up on the physical side of love. You know, if your mom was google-eyed, had a hair lip, with one tooth in her mouth and a goatee, I would still love her."

There is a pause as Vivianna and Bobby both look at each other and reject the claim simultaneously, "Nah!"

The family reaches the car. Vivianna is busy placing Sula in her car seat. Kwamina and Bobby are at the back of the car waiting for traffic to clear before getting in.

Bobby whispers, "Son, tomorrow is our wedding anniversary and your mama thinks I've forgotten. Boy is she gonna be surprised. I'm setting her up. Don't tell her anything, not one word!"

Kwamina acknowledges with excitement, "Okay, Dad, I promise…our secret," giving his father dap.

Everyone settles into the car. Bobby checks the traffic and pulls out. He sighs and addresses Kwamina, "Feelings of love—the most powerful force in our universe Son. Love has started and ended wars—a true gift from God. The highest of all highs, it's like Christmas morning every day."

Hakeem blurts out, "I like Christmas."

"Sure, because of the good feelings and anticipation it brings."

"No, toys!"

Bobby is interrupted by a loud horn. A cabby cuts him off. He shouts, "I love you too," and resumes his conversation. "Love needs your attention every moment. You work with it to keep it alive. In its purest form it's unconditional."

Kwamina asks, "Meaning?"

"Meaning whatever comes with it is accepted as part of it. If I'm fat, that's fine; or if I'm ugly or not so smart, that's fine too. You accept the person for what's in their heart regardless of other things."

Vivianna interjects sarcastically, "And if you're forgetful?" She is starting to resent his lapse of memory. Bobby nods in agreement. Kwamina makes eye contact with Bobby in the rear view mirror and they offer each other a wink.

"Do you understand, Son?"

"Yeah."

Hakeem spots a fine woman and says, "Boy, I could love her."

"Dad, what's up with this kid?"

"That's not love son, that's just lust. I wasn't aware you could get it that young. Don't worry Kwam, in time, I'll teach him how to keep that in check." Bobby gives Hakeem that look, "Boy, I've got my work cut out for me."

Hakeem gives his father a dismissing wave.

Putting her book down, Vivianna warns, "Kwam be careful. As good as love feels…well, it can hurt just as badly. We live in a world of opposing factors Son," then continues to read.

"Love completes the circle of life Son; it reciprocates. To love and to be loved makes it complete; it takes two. Life without love is merely existing, but life with abundant love is TRULY living. Now, on the other handĺ, there is the expression of love—how you show it. Take for instance the words 'I love you.' Sometimes it's hard for people to say it, but they may feel it and really just can't say the words. In those cases, you read body language, gestures, terms of endearment, and the like. I, on the other hand, witnessed the love of my parents and learned from them. Because of that, it makes it so easy for me to love and hug my family in expressions of love for you. It's a form of affection—a very affectionate love."

"What's terms of endearment Dad?"

"Something else you may call somebody you care about like a personal nickname. I was your mother's Boobutsi, and she was my Tututa, and this was how we addressed each other."

"Boobutsi—sick!"

Hakeem sticks his finger in his mouth, "Tututa!"

Vivianna shakes her head and lowers it in shame. Smiling, she adds, "Your dad had another name—pissy, pissy, pole cat, because he wet the bed until he was twelve years old."

Kwamina asks, "Really Dad?"

"Yeah. We could never figure it out; but they didn't make an issue of it. Mama and daddy would wash my sheets routinely without any fuss. They loved me so much that they accepted me with all of my problems."

Hakeem looks on in disbelief.

"Suppose I wet the bed like you Daddy?"

"The love I feel for you is unconditional, but what we'd probably do is sell you to the highest bidder or give you away."

"You're kidding huh Dad?"

Vivianna adds, "Or make you pay half the laundry bills."

"Foolish pride, that's another thing. Foolish pride can destroy love when you can't humble yourself to situations in love. Honey, how much do you love me?" Bobby asks while taunting Vivianna.

"Just enough to keep from killing you."

Bobby and Kwamina laugh. Hakeem shakes his head from side to side.

Sula becomes worried, "Mama don't kill my daddy."

"Oh no Baby. I won't; I'm only kidding sugar." Vivianna returns to reading.

"See Son, don't put off expressions of love; let it flow like a mighty river."

"And what about sharing love Mr. Expert?"

"Oh yeah, sharing love unselfishly...I'm glad you reminded me Tututa."

The family continues to drive down a busy New York street with the usual activity—pedestrians, traffic, street noises, etc.

"That's a gift to be shared by all. When two people love each other they live for each other's happiness; you don't think of yourself. Your mom and I shared our love and you three are a direct result of that love— the physical aspect especially." Bobby gives Vivianna a look. She is aware that he is trying to make eye contact, but she continues to ignore him. She looks out the car window. "Kwamina, I'll discuss this with you later in more detail."

"No real need to Dad. We read all about sex and reproduction in class."

"Great! Anything you don't understand?"

"Um...I'm okay".

"Son, sex is one thing, but parenting is an unending job, like love. Having children is a very challenging and a very rewarding experience; and there are sacrifices. Sometimes you're tested to do things you don't want to do, but you do them anyway. You sacrifice your feelings and do exactly what needs to be done. That is, as long as it is legal and no one gets hurt."

"For example Dad?"

"Like when your mother drags me to bingo with all those old ladies smelling like Ben gay and mothballs. I'm not particularly fond of bingo, but I love making your mother happy. So, I make the sacrifice and I go. It's all about sacrifices Son. Dr. King sacrificed his life for our rights, just as Jesus sacrificed his life to save our souls. In my line of work, my life means nothing if someone's life is in danger. I just have to react and pray we both survive. All good deeds are rewarded somehow or another."

Bobby pulls up to a stop light as two gay men are crossing the street hand in hand. "Now you see that. A figure of speech is to share your love with your fellow man, but these guys are taking it to another level. But love is good no matter how you express it. Now those are some loving people once you get to know them. Of course, I don't condone what they do, but I don't judge or condemn them either. That's only because they're human beings who deserve to be loved and understood."

The gay men observe Bobby noticing them and give him a feminine wave. He returns the same kind of wave and looks at Vivianna, whose eyes are wide. She is smiling, and despite her reluctance to smile, she gives in to laughter.

"Apply logic to everyday life to help you make decisions. Remember, God made women to reproduce with a hole with a purpose, and He made a man with a pole with a purpose."

"Must you be so graphic Bobby?"

"Viv, the boy already knows what's going on. Don't look at the surface, look within. Look for heart in a person and see all people as valued human beings."

Hakeem once again feels left out of the conversation. "I like red beans. Mom, can you fix me some of those human beings? Will they give me gas like this?" Hakeem leans forward to expel gas for attention. Kwamina and Vivianna immediately attempt to roll down their windows. Bobby, anticipating their move, presses the auto lock button and locks the windows while backing into their parking spot.

Kwamina pleads, "Dad, no…this is torture! Please Dad it's burning my eyes!"

Sula is fanning her face.

Vivianna clenches her teeth and demands, "Bobby Washington put these windows down now!" She slowly and methodically puts her book down, turns around, and gives Hakeem that look. Hakeem smiles and looks away. As soon as the car comes to a complete stop, everyone bails. Vivianna gets out of the car saying, "I swear that stench is in my clothes." Sula is choking as Bobby runs to her rescue. Hakeem is smart enough to stay out of striking distance by walking ahead of everyone else. The family walks to their apartment.

Kwamina embraces his father and asks, "Dad, how do you know when you're in love?"

"I don't know, that's a little bit harder to explain. It'll make you do foolish things. I remember humming this little song 'I'm at the top of the world, looking down on creation' by the Carpenter's. Yeah, your mom used to laugh at me, but I hummed it all the time. It was like I was really in tune with so much when I hummed it, as if I had a seventh sense that allowed me to feel things I hadn't felt before. Silly songs stayed in my head and sappy movies made me cry. It kinda throws a man's balance off. Beautiful love songs had meaning back then. I'd listen to the lyrics. I could feel the songs. Your mom and I had our special song, and most couples had their special song." At this point, Bobby looks at Vivianna for acknowledgement, but she is really pouting. "It's like all your God given senses are intensified at that point. You know something is happening to you. But, like I said earlier, you can't really explain it. You just really kind of know it."

"There's this white girl at school who is always hitting me. What's that all about Dad?"

"My boy—"

"She's everywhere I go. I turn around and there she is looking at me when she's not close enough to strike me. It's kinda weird and kinda funny at the same time."

"Sounds like you're her first love."

"What? I have to marry her?"

Laughing, Bobby explains, "No, no, no, Son. She's just attracted to you and she's not quite sure how to express those feelings she's having. This is something she'll learn in time as she gets older, as she witnesses the love of her parents, and as she's taught how to love."

"We have to be taught how to love?"

"Oh yeah, how to love as well as how to hate; they're both taught. It's just not natural. Little babies don't know how to hate until they see their parents interact with other people. Children from a loving two-parent family have a much better chance of survival and achievement than those who are less fortunate. God and logic are the foundation for a good life."

The family arrives at their apartment building. Kwamina says, "Mom, I'll be up for supper." Kwamina greets his friends and takes a seat on the steps with a few girls. Bobby observes his son interacting with them.

As Bobby enters the apartment Vivianna is drilling Hakeem on the Ten Commandments. Sula is trying hard to keep up. Hakeem eventually gets stuck on one of the commandments and becomes frustrated. "Mom, you know none of these are for kids, so why do I have to learn them now?"

Vivianna doesn't respond, but gives him that nerve taking, earth shattering look.

Hakeem nervously blurts out, "Thou shalt not kill!"

Meanwhile, a group of boys led by Calvin, the neighborhood bully, taunts Kwamina because they are jealous of the attention he is receiving from the girls.

Calvin slyly says, "Think you all that?" He throws his football at Kwamina. Kwamina catches it and stands up. As he stands, the girls egg him on to fight.

Anya instigates, "Ohhh!"

Maya asks, "Kwam you gonna take that?"

"Calvin, the way you threw that ball, I would think you were trying to hurt me." Kwamina walks down the stairs toward Calvin as the girls continue to instigate the imminent fight.

Jaycee is shadow boxing.

Anya urges, "Go get him, Kwam!"

Maya removes her earrings and says, "We got your back."

"Oh no, I got this."

Calvin taunts Kwamina, "And what...you bad now?" as he gestures to Kwamina. "Bring it on...come on. You wanna piece of me? Show me what you got. Come take your best shot."

The kids playing in the street begin to circle the boys, who are about to fight. Calvin outweighs Kwamina by a few pounds and is a couple of years older. Kwamina fearlessly thinks to himself, David and Goliath, but no sling shot, so I'll have to use that old sucker punch. The crowd is getting very anxious. Kwamina looks at the spot on Calvin's jaw where he needs to make contact. Kwamina looks up and calls Calvin's mother's name, "Mrs. Coleman!"

Calvin looks up and Kwamina delivers a strong right hook to the jaw. He pulls all the way back from his right shoulder and BAM! Calvin staggers back and Kwamina knows that it is now or never. Kwamina pounces on Calvin and the crowd is screaming. Vivianna hears the commotion downstairs and looks out the window.

"Bobby, Kwam's fighting!"

Bobby leaps from the sofa and rushes downstairs. When he gets to the stoop, he stops and sees Kwamina over Calvin, waylaying him. Bobby yells in his resonating baritone voice, getting everyone's attention. "Kwamina!"

The Earth stops, Kwamina stops. Calvin is trying to protect his face from another right hook that stops in mid air.

"The demons of violence and hate are in control of you. Their talons dig deep into your soul. Shake them off! Rebuke them now Kwamina Washington."

Vivianna and Hakeem are looking down from the apartment window as Sula desperately jumps up to get a peek at the action below. Bobby's voice brings an instant hush over the crowd. Calvin's mother appears with Smukie, the neighborhood thief. Everyone sees him, and then grabs and checks their valuables.

Mrs. Coleman screams at Bobby, "Get him off my boy!"

Bobby gestures, showing her the palm of his hands. He addresses Kwamina, "Be a real man and end this now."

Kwamina stands and reaches for Calvin. Calvin puts his guard up, thinking Kwamina is about to deliver another blow. Instead, Kwamina helps him to his feet, brushing him off. "Sorry, Man, you're welcome to come and talk to us."

"I know. I guess I got jealous. You're all those girls ever talk about. They think you're so smart and I feel so dumb."

"Confused at times, but not dumb my brother."

Calvin tries to smile, but his mouth hurts; he grimaces. They give each other a hood handshake. Bobby turns to leave.

"Get over here boy!" Mrs. Coleman yells while slapping Calvin upside the head.

"Ouch! What's that for?"

"For letting that little boy whip your big ass!"

Smukie runs over to Kwamina as the girls brush his clothing and pat his back in congratulations. "Kwamina, you and me can be a team! Man, you pick the fight and get the crowd going while I work them you know. I'll let my fingers do the walking, I'll meet you later, and we can split everything down the middle."

Kwamina, fixing his clothes, looks Smukie dead in the eyes and says, "No!"

Bobby returns upstairs where Sula meets him at the top of the landing with arms wide open. Bobby picks her up. Hakeem is in the kitchen helping his mother prepare supper.

Sula pleads as she jumps up and down, "Daddy, will you please have a tea party with me...pretty, pretty, pretty please?"

"You must have been reading my mind sweetheart. That's just what I was thinking."

Sula proceeds to put makeup and a tattered blonde wig on her father. When he's made up to her satisfaction, she holds her princess mirror up for him. "What do you think, Dad? Oh no, not dad. I think I'll name you Lady B." Seated at Sula's play table, they start their tea party, speaking with strong British accents.

"And I shall call you your highness, my queen of hearts."

"Lady B, I'm so glad you could join me for tea."

"Your highness, I am truly honored to have been invited to your castle for tea."

At this moment, Kwamina enters and sees his dad. He falls to his knees, holding his stomach with laughter. Hearing the commotion, Hakeem enters the room, witnesses the hilarious sight before him, and joins Kwamina on the floor, kicking. Vivianna looks in from the kitchen, shaking her head in disbelief, she laughs.

Kwamina laughs, "Dad, what are you doing?"

"No pride and sacrifice for love. I'm having tea with your highness, the queen of hearts."

Sula addresses Kwamina, "Bow before your queen."

Bowing, Kwamina says, "Your highness," looking at his dad, "your madness, please excuse me to my chambers."

"Proceed," she says while pointing.

Bobby says, "Your highness, did I fail to mention how smashingly stunning your dress is?"

"It's a bloody good thing you did because I was about to have you beheaded." Sula runs her fingers across her neck while making a gurgling sound.

Bobby gives her a surprised look. "Enjoy your tea."

As they exaggeratedly sip tea from the toy teacups, the doorbell rings. Vivianna runs toward the door, "Got it." She answers the door and Dave, a fellow fireman and lifelong friend of Bobby's, enters. They greet each other with a hug and a kiss on the cheek.

"Vivianna, marry me. Let me take you away from this."

"Keep on asking, you might get lucky."

"You know if I had my own key I could let myself in."

Dave notices Vivianna's sullen mood. "I don't like that look. What's the matter?"

"Oh nothing," she sighs.

"Vivianna, I'm the only person on Earth besides Bobby who really knows you. So what's up?"

"Well tomorrow is our fifteenth wedding anniversary and Bobby hasn't mentioned a thing about it. I really think he forgot; that's all."

"You know he has a lot on his mind lately with the program he's spearheading at the firehouse for the kids—you know...the drug awareness program and those CPR classes."

"Yeah, just like a friend, you'll make excuses for your boy." Dave shrugs his shoulders and smiles. Approaching the top of the stairs, Vivianna whispers to him. "Dave, you have got to see this. Stay here and peek in. I'm going to leave the door open."

Bowing from his knees, Dave agrees, "Okay."

Vivianna enters the apartment unnoticed. Dave is taking in the funniest sight he has seen in a long time—his best friend made up, playing with his daughter. Dave falls in on the floor kicking with laughter as Bobby hurriedly tries to remove the makeup and wig. Dave finally composes himself as Bobby looks at him with disgust. Dave bows to Queen Sula and acknowledges Lady B. "My ladies, allow me the pleasure of telling you how beautiful you are tonight."

Bobby reaches for Dave, who outmaneuvers him and escapes.

Dave sniffs the air, "Mmm, gumbo."

Sula adds, "My mama can cook some bood bumbo," waving her hand and sucking her teeth. "Um, well, you know what I mean."

Vivianna says, "You're welcome to stay for dinner Dave, there's plenty."

"Um, okay!" he hesitates playfully.

Hakeem sets the table.

Vivianna praises him, "Thank you my little prince." She then shuttles food in from the kitchen. After she is seated, everyone holds hands to say grace.

Bobby says grace, "Jehovah God, we thank thee for this food we are about to receive. We thank you for all the other bountiful blessings you have bestowed upon us—a strong roof over our heads, love, and happy hearts. Dear and kind God, merciful Father, thank you for life, thank you for family, and thank you for true friends,"making eye contact with Dave. "Thank you for this food lest we forget those who are less fortunate. We ask that you feed them Father, the food and grace they need to live. Amen."

Everyone chimes in, "Amen."

Vivianna serves Sula while everyone else serves themselves. They all marvel over the delectable gumbo.

Bobby changes the subject, "We met this kid in the park today, um—"

Kwamina excitedly interjects, "J!"

"Yes, Dave, you wouldn't believe this kid's arm. Reminds me—"

"Remind you?" Vivianna interrupts.

Bobby gives her a quick glance then returns to Dave.

Dave adds, "Yes, reminds me of those high school games, remember?"

Vivianna can't resist the sarcasm, "Remember?"

It's obvious the two men and Kwamina know what she's doing. Bobby makes eye contact with Kwamina and they wink at each other. Vivianna makes eye contact with Dave, who shrugs and looks away.

"Boy, do I remember," Dave says, "How can I live down that last district game?"

Bobby laughs, "I hope you never live it down. I hope you suffer forever."

Kwamina anxiously asks, "What happened?"

Vivianna groans, "Oh no, I don't want to hear this story again. This has got to be number three hundred."

Kwamina begs, "Uncle Dave, number three-o-one for me please."

"I'll let your dad tell it. You know how he can exaggerate."

Bobby pushes back from his food. He places his chin in clenched fists, looking into space and shaking his head back and forth, smiling. "It was a must win game, our ticket to the playoffs. We were down by two. It was forth and long with three seconds left on the clock, and nowhere near field goal range—unless we had Tom Dempsey on our team. But, back to reality, we had my arm and Uncle Dave's hands."

Kwamina and Hakeem listen intensely, looking directly at Bobby. Bobby looks at Dave who gestures him to finish. "Oh no, go right ahead."

"The ball is snapped. Uncle Dave makes a move on his defender, nothing fancy, but the guy trips and falls. Uncle Dave is all alone. I'll tell you, he was in tight end abyss, all by himself. I then let go one of the most perfectly spiraled precision passes of my entire career; knowing that the scouts were going to rush to the field in a few moments to recruit me to some Ivy League College or HBCU."

Hakeem asks, "What's an HBCU?"

Kwamina answers proudly, "Historical Black College or University."

"The ball was in slow motion and people were cheering. Half the stadium was empty; the opponents left. That fast, I mean it—Uncle Dave had time to go to the stand, buy a hot dog, and still catch that ball."

Hakeem laughs. Kwamina eggs on his dad.

"And then...and then?"

There is silence while everyone waits.

Sula yells, "He dropped it!"

Everyone laughs.

Kwamina, in disbelief says, "Oh no, Uncle Dave… no Uncle Dave."

Dave gives a fast up and down shake of the head, gesturing in agreement. "Yep…but look…stop laughing so I can tell you what happened. I mean, if you really want to know."

Bobby and Vivianna look at each other curiously. Vivianna puts her spoon down and says, "I gotta hear this after all these years."

Dave looks Bobby squarely in the eyes. "I dropped that ball for you buddy."

"What?"

"That's right. I did it for you. What was going through my mind while that ball was coming to me like the Good Year Blimp was, who would the scouts run to after that game to recruit? For our friendship, I didn't want to steal your glory."

"You no catching lying dog. You couldn't catch a good cold!" Bobby says as he roars with laughter.

Everyone laughs and goes back to their meals. The meal is ending and everyone is praising Vivianna.

Dave compliments, "Vivianna, you could cook a fireman's boot and I'd eat it girl!"

Bobby retorts, "She wouldn't have to add any cheese to your boots!"

Hakeem teases, "Speaking of cheese, I'm gonna squeeze mine," as he toots up to the side to pass gas. Vivianna gives him that look and Hakeem immediately excuses himself to the bathroom where they can clearly hear him.

Sula admits, "I would rather hear it than smell it."

"Hakeem, Sula, it's time for bed," their mother states.

Dave volunteers, "Okay you two, get ready for bed and I'll tuck you in." Looking at Bobby and Vivianna, he says, "I'll take care of that."

Vivianna passes Bobby on her way to the kitchen. She makes eye contact with him and cuts her eyes. Bobby smiles and continues to channel surf. Dave walks over to the couch and rests his head on Bobby's shoulder. Bobby immediately pushes his head away. "I told you I'm not like that."

"Couldn't convince me earlier with that pretty blonde wig and make up on."

"You know, come to think of it, most of your girl-friends did have facial hairs. Remember Mona...mus-tache Mona? That was a girl wasn't it?" Bobby teases.

"Aaah, man. That's cold blooded!" Dave looks toward the kitchen to see if Vivianna is listening. He turns to Bobby and whispers, "Hey dummy, do you know what tomorrow is?"

"Sunday you idiot!"

Dave looks over toward the kitchen again and turns back to Bobby. "No, no—" Before he could say anything else, Bobby whispers.

"It's my anniversary."

"Just checking." In a loud voice he says, "I'll go tuck my kids in."

Hakeem and Sula share a bunk—Hakeem on top and Sula on bottom by the window. Kwamina has his own bed against the opposite wall with a mural of great men—Dr. King, Malcolm X, President Kennedy, Gandhi, and a black Jesus. Dave enters the room and notices Sula struggling to open the window.

"Uncle Dave, help me with this?"

"¬Su Su, why are we raising this window? It's cold out!"

"I have to put out some feed so my children can have breakfast in the morning."

"Children?"

"Yeah Uncle Dave, my pet pigeons."

"Oh, okay".

"This row is for General Lee, this one is for General Grant, and this one is for General Davis."

"Lee? Grant? Davis? Lee and Grant I know."

"Yeah, from that war…they are always fighting. And Davis is the best flyer—a Tuskegee Airman. You should see him Uncle Dave. Kwam says he was the first black general."

"Oh, okay".

"I love you Uncle Dave," Sula says innocently as she wraps her arms around his neck.

Smiling broadly and kissing her on the forehead, he adds, "And I love you too, Su Su." Dave tucks Sula in then stands up to tuck in Hakeem, who is in deep thought.

"Hakeem what are you thinking about?"

Hakeem is lying on his back, looking up at the ceiling. "Well Uncle Dave, I have this science project tomorrow that I'd like to demonstrate for you."

"Great. I'd love to see it."

"Oh, well, you'll do more than see it. Reach me that baby powder please." Hakeem reaches for the powder and pours some in his pajama pants. He positions himself on his hands and knees facing Dave and cuts loose a loud one. Dave is amazed at the cloud of powder that blows from the back of Hakeem's pants.

Hakeem, hysterical, falls flat on the bed. Dave is weak from laughter. "Uncle Dave, I call that the three O's," Hakeem says, pinching his nose, "smelly-o," pointing to his ears, "audio," and flashing his palms near his eyes, "video."

Dave nudges him and tucks him in. "OKAY Stinkinstein...time to go to sleep-o." As Dave approaches Kwamina's bed, he notices he is reading a book about Dr. Martin Luther King Jr. Kwamina sees Dave approaching and slams his book shut.

"You're not coming to tuck me in are you?"

"Oh no, but what are you reading?"

"Dr. King's Letter from a Birmingham Jail."

Dave makes room on the edge of the bed and takes notice of the mural on Kwamina's wall. "There's one great man missing from your wall."

"Who?" Kwamina asks, as he put his book down.

"Your dad. Let me tell you something about your dad. He's been my best friend most of my life. From high school to the military, we joined together—the buddy system. We did a tour of duty in Vietnam and now the fire department. I followed him to the fire department. I owe him my life."

"Why?"

"It was in Kom Tune province on the Ho Chi Minh Trail through the thick jungle. Your dad and I were with Bravo company recon. I had just taken point, when suddenly, your dad pulled me back by the ruck sack! I fell on my ass. I asked him what the problem was. His answer was, 'I'm going to need you later in life and we are going home together from this war.' My first thought was that he was losing it. Then he picked up a tree branch and threw it a few feet in front of me on the trail. There was this sudden loud snap and a booby trap was sprung! A bamboo stick with six razor sharp daggers tied to it shot in the path I was just about to step in. I would have been impaled on those daggers. They would have gone right through me. And what's worse is that you don't die instantly, it's slow and agonizing. Your dad saved my life and I owe him. But you know him, he hates it when I say I owe him." Dave tears up and solemnly looks away.

Kwamina touches his shoulder. "How can there be so much hate in this world?"

"Kwam, I don't know. We can't right all the wrong in this world. Let's just write our page in the Book of Life." They give each other a soul shake and Dave leaves for the living room.

Dave joins his friend on the sofa. He snatches the remote control and changes the channel as Bobby reaches for it. Dave holds the remote out of Bobby's reach, changing the channels back and forth like a little kid. Dave gets up and Bobby chases him around the sofa. Bobby, frustrated, stops and throws a pillow at Dave, who drops the remote. Trying to catch the pillow, he drops that also. Bobby dives onto the sofa after the remote and Dave dives on top of him.

Irritated, Vivianna asks, "Why don't you two knock it off so the kids can get to sleep?" She throws a dishtowel at them and returns to the kitchen.

Bobby and Dave struggle to catch their breath. Bobby says jokingly, "Dropped that pillow huh? Still can't catch anything and hold onto it!"

"Yeah, I guess you're right. Can't even catch a woman; and when I do, I always drop them," Dave adds while yawning.

"More like, they drop you. You're tired; isn't it time for you to go home?" Bobby asks while nodding toward the door.

"Naaah, I want to watch some TV."

Bobby gives Dave a look and then gestures his head toward Vivianna in the kitchen. "I know it's time for you to go home."

Dave finally takes the hint, "Yeah, yeah, okay. Good night Vivianna; thanks again for the gumbo. Dave hits Bobby on the fist. "See you tomorrow partner. I'll see myself out."

Vivianna enters the room, drying her hands. She says, "You're welcome, anytime."

"Don't tell him that."

"I'll see myself out."

Bobby, realizing they are alone, seizes the moment to romance his wife. He walks into the kitchen and hugs her around the waist from behind. She tries to squirm out of his arms. "Go ahead on boyee. Leave me alone, yeah."

"Vivianna, you know what that does to me when you speak that Creole talk." Bobby wets his lips then kisses the nape of her neck.

Vivianna melts and breathes deeply, "Ohhh mon cheri, tu cownnais monpoint faible." (Ohhh, my love, you know my weak spot.)

Bobby breaks away from Vivianna and says, "I have a surprise for you."

Vivianna anticipates a gift, thinking he has remembered their anniversary. She dries her hands hurriedly, smiles broadly, and walks into the living room. When the music hits her, it is their song "Close Your Eyes," by Aaron Neville and Linda Ronstadt. Vivianna can sing;

Bobby cannot, but he does the best he can. They embrace and slow dance in each other's arms. Suddenly, Bobby notices the boys peeping in from their bedroom. He gestures to Vivianna. She starts to say something to them when Bobby covers her mouth; his eyes tell her not to say a thing. They end the song.

"I love you Bobby with all my heart and soul."

Bobby embraces her and gives her a passionate kiss. She leans back, looking him in the eyes, then looks down between them. "What's this?"

"Looks like a rat crawled between us."

She laughs, looking away. Vivianna then looks back at Bobby. "I have just the trap for that rat."

They head toward the bedroom, stop together, look over their shoulders, and address the boys. "Good night boys." Surprised, Hakeem and Kwamina dash to their beds.

CHAPTER 2

A Tragic Loss

It is Sunday morning. The sun is shining and the gospel song "This Little Light of Mine" is being played softly in the background. Sula is half dressed and playing with her pigeons on the windowsill. Kwamina is dressing Hakeem. Bobby is in uniform, paying particular attention to the stock exchange section of the morning paper. Vivianna walks through the apartment looking for her gift. Bobby looks over the top of the paper and smiles at his wife. When she does not find what she is looking for, she slams the oven door shut.

In exasperation she mutters, "Senile cheap sucker!"

Sula runs to Bobby to button her dress and he notices her shoes are on the wrong feet. Bobby buttons her dress and seats her on the table in front of him so that he can correct her shoes. "You know, you're as beautiful as your mother." Bobby looks toward Vivianna in the kitchen. She makes eye contact long enough to cut her eyes and then continues with her baking. Sula puts her father's uniform hat on as the boys rush in from dressing.

Hakeem excitedly asks, "How do we look Dad?"

"Like two distinguished gentlemen I'm very proud of." The boys make funny gestures of pride. Bobby places Sula on the floor and removes his hat from her head. "I love the company but I've got a job to get to honey." Bobby kisses Sula on the neck, tickling her. He then hugs Hakeem and kisses him on the forehead. As Bobby approaches Kwamina, the boy holds his arms up to shield his face.

"Come on, Dad. I'm too old for that."

While gathering his gear, Bobby says, "Son, you're never too old to express your love for someone. True love supersedes age, race, religion, and social status. Don't let society dictate your freedom of expression." Pointing his finger, he continues, "You be an exception to the rule." Bobby turns and walks to the door hoping Vivianna will be there for their customary kiss good-bye. When it's obvious she is not coming, he goes into the kitchen to kiss her. Instead of kissing him directly, she offers her cheek. He looks into her eyes with a hint of sorrow. "Goodbye Vivianna."

She seems confused, shakes off the tremor, and goes back to her pies, sensing something was strange about that goodbye. Vivianna enters the living room and says, "Kwamina, tell Father Pete I'm missing mass today because I'm still working on the pies for the social this evening. I got a late start." Vivianna walks over to the window when Hakeem vexes her by asking a stupid question.

"Can I stay and help with the pies?"

She looks out the window just as Bobby is about to get into the car. He feels her looking down on him. He looks up and they make eye contact. He mouths the words, "I love you."

Vivianna only responds with clenched lips and re-directs her attention back to the kids.

Bobby arrives at the firehouse and notices Jeremiah sitting against the building. He obviously has been there a while, probably even overnight. "How long have you been here J?"

Jeremiah rubs his eyes, as if just waking up. He is wearing the same clothes he had on the previous day, which have a hint of being homeless.

Stuttering, Jeremiah replies, "Mr. Bobby, I...I...I just wanted to make sure this was the right firehouse. I asked them last night—" Catching himself, and trying to cover with a lie, he says, "Uh, I just asked them inside and they said you'd actually be here this morning. And I...I just didn't want to miss you."

Not buying his story, Bobby replies, "Okay J, let's head inside." Jeremiah follows Bobby into the fire-house where Bobby is greeted by the other firemen as "Lady B."

A fireman jokes in a high pitched voice, "Oh Lady B...your ladyship, so pleased you could make it down to the fire station today."

Another fireman adds, "Yes, could we offer you a spot of tea perhaps?"

Bobby, embarrassed, says, "All right you guys. Knock it off. Where is he? I'm going to kill him!"

When Dave walks into the room, Bobby chases him around the table. Both of them stop as soon as the cap-tain appears.

Fire Captain Bonner admonishes, "Bobby, Dave, knock it off. And who is this?"

A third fireman, Kevin, is in the background prepar-ing breakfast; some breakfast is already on the table.

"This is my—"

Jeremiah interrupts, "Son."

Bobby plays along, "Yeah, okay, Kevin, can you hook him up?"

"Sure thing; coming right up."

Jeremiah, without hesitation, makes his way to the breakfast table and dives right in. Bobby and Dave watch Jeremiah; it is obvious he hasn't eaten in days.

Dave asks, "Is this the J?"

"Oh, yeah."

Dave extends his hand, but Jeremiah doesn't notice because he is gorging his breakfast with both hands. "Oh okay, just continue eating," Dave said while chuckling.

Fire Captain Bonner adds, "Bobby there's a room full of kids waiting for you."

When Bobby and Dave walk into the large room, the kids start cheering for them. Dave is making funny gestures like a prize fighter. Bobby tries to quiet everyone, "Alright, alright, let's calm down. Now, may I direct your attention to the blackboard? These are your CPR instructions. Now remember, these are very serious. It may be the difference between life and death. We're going to review some procedures now. As soon as Kevin comes in we are going to have a little demonstration."

Kevin enters the room and says, "I can't find that damn practice dummy."

Concerned, Bobby asks, "What are we gonna use for a dummy?" Everyone simultaneously looks at Dave.

Embarrassed, Dave says, "Ah, come on. Give me a break, okay". Dave assumes the position flat on his back. Bobby approaches Dave and explains what to notice about his victim.

"Shake the victim and shout for a response. If there is no response, shout for help. When help arrives, send them to call 911. Open the airway by lifting the chin and gently pushing down on the forehead. Once this is done, put your ear close to the victim's mouth. Look for chest movement and listen for the sound of breathing. Feel for breath on your cheek. The best way to give rescue breathing is by using the mouth-to-mouth technique. Nose pinched, chin lifted, and two full breaths mouth-to-mouth." When Bobby moves his head into position to demonstrate mouth-to-mouth, Dave pulls Bobby's head down in one swift motion, placing his hand between his and Bobby's lips. The kids do not see Dave's hand from their angle. Dave makes a loud smacking sound.

"I swear…his hand was there! His hand was there!" Bobby says, very embarrassed.

Dave replies in a feminine voice, "It was not," standing and hitting Bobby's arm, "it really wasn't!" addressing the kids.

"Dave you're a fool. You play too much and this is no joking matter. We're trying to teach these kids something."

Dave does his Hardy impression, trying to cry on Bobby's chest. Bobby pushes him away.

One child says excitedly, "Let's dance!"

Bobby agrees, "Hey, that's a great idea. Now, who can tell me the fireman's theme song?"

The children all yell, "Fire!"

A little girl with one hand on her hip snaps her fingers and says, "By the Ohio Players."

The song is cued on the boom box very loudly. The kids dance and Dave attempts to dance. The kids have a big laugh. Suddenly, the fire alarm sounds. The music is immediately turned off. Everyone listens and some children try to quiet the others. The children put their fingers to their lips. "Shhh…"

Bobby and Dave listen intensely for the address of the fire.

The Fire Dispatcher announces, "Fire alarm—a three-alarm zone 702—engine five, engine twenty-seven, engine fifty-three, ladder seven, ladder forty-three, battalion chief thirty-seven. Please respond to a phone alarm at 200 E. 104th, cross street Lexington. Location, in building. Report, smoke alarm third floor."

Bobby calls out, "Kevin, take care of the kids. We should be back in a couple of hours."

Firemen come from everywhere, sliding down the poles and running to put on their turn out gear and position themselves in their prospective units. The captain reaches the cab the same time as Bobby and 10-8's the roll. The captain looks at Bobby, who says, "I know exactly where it is." The doors roll up.

Bobby notices Jeremiah standing by the driver's door. Bobby gives Jeremiah a quick glance and a wink. "I'll be right back Son."

Jeremiah gives Bobby a broad smile, a wink, and a thumbs up. As Bobby pulls out, Jeremiah runs alongside his unit to the street. As the pumper and ladder unit advance and make the right turn, Jeremiah directs them. The sirens, lights, and horns blare. The unit makes a left turn onto the street; the fire is about two blocks away. Smoke is pouring from the third floor of a building with visible flames.

Fire Captain Bonner instructs, "Give Dave a flying stretch."

Bobby points to the fire hydrant he expects Dave to use.

Fire Captain Bonner says, "Fire alarm, this is Engine fifty-three. I need more units...strike a box."

Bobby stops the truck just long enough for Dave to reposition himself behind the unit and grab the end of the fire hose. A news crew in the immediate area hears the dispatch over their scanners and responds. When Dave has a firm grip on the fire hose, Bobby takes off, stopping the fire engine strategically in front of the burning building. The captain gives orders to the firemen; Bobby knows what to do.

"You two guys man that hose and send some water to the third floor." Speaking over the radio he says, "Let's get that snorkel unit in position. We have to get the ladder unit in closer."

Bobby pulls, pushes, set dials, hooks up the water supply line, and gives Dave the signal to send the water. The hose inflates. The firemen brace themselves, anticipating the pressure. Several police units are arriving for traffic and crowd control. The front line of tenants who have escaped the fire come out to the established line. Smoke is pouring all over; water is applied. The news crew and ambulances arrive. Cameras roll and the reporter sets up to interview the captain.

Reporter Connie Anderson asks, "Is everyone out of the building?"

Fire Captain Bonner responds, "To the best of my knowledge. We have a search and rescue unit on the way."

"Any idea of what may have caused the fire?"

"We haven't determined that yet but we have established it's contained to the third floor."

Inside the apartment on the television, an anchor team mentions the fire and the live news crew on location is preparing to transmit.

News Anchor Phil Martin reports, "Phil Martin here, we interrupt your regular scheduled program to bring you a live report on a three-alarm fire that just broke out in Spanish Harlem. We switch live to Connie Anderson who is on the scene. Connie…"

Vivianna sees the report, but passes on through the room, picking up a few things. She goes into the kitchen to check on her pies.

Back at the fire scene, a woman pushes her way through the crowd. When she reaches the front, she goes around the barricade, frantically searching for someone. The police try to subdue her, but she breaks away, running to a girl with a baby in her arms and holding a toddler by the hand.

Maritza frantically asks, "Where's Amanda?"

The babysitter replies, "She was in the back playing when we left the building."

Maritza pushes through the crowd to a police officer and frantically explains her plight. "I think my little girl is in the back."

"Ma'am, please stay here. Calm down. I'll go check."

Maritza hesitates for a moment then runs past the officer toward the rear of the building. When they do not find the child, she panics and runs around to the front of the building and tries to enter. The firemen make an attempt to stop her, but she fights them, kicking and screaming. *"Mi nina! Mi nina! Amanda,*

Amanda! Quiera mi nina" (My daughter! My daughter! Amanda, Amanda! I want my daughter.)

Bobby notices Maritza and addresses a tenant. "What's going on?"

"She's the Spanish lady who lives on the third floor, apartment 301." The tenant points and everybody looks up. "She has three children."

"What's she screaming about?"

Another tenant pleads, "Save her baby. One of them is still in there."

In the interim, Vivianna glances at the television and sees Bobby's back. She pauses, and establishes he is okay. With the thought of him being in danger, her anger subsides. She then decides to call the firehouse.

Kevin answers, "Engine company fifty-three, watchman Kevin speaking."

"Hi Kevin, this is Vivianna Washington. I just saw the news. Please have Bobby call me when he returns."

"No problem Mrs. Washington. Everything is going well at the fire scene. Bobby should be back in a couple of hours. I'll have him call you."

"Thank you Kevin."

"Bye."

"Goodbye."

Back at the fire, Bobby notices two firemen listening to his conversation; he gives them a look and gestures. They look at each other and walk away. Bobby realizes the firemen are not going in to attempt the rescue of this child, so he puts on his gear.

Fire Captain Bonner asks, "Bobby what do you think you're doing?"

"I believe there's a child in 301. I'm going in," he explains, while grabbing his oxygen tank.

"You're not supposed to go in there Bobby." When Bobby turns away, the captain grabs him, looking him in the eyes. "Bobby, I order you to return to your post."

"I can't. I am ordered by a higher power." He makes the sign of the cross after pulling away and dashes in through the doorway of the burning building. The crowd gasps. Maritza is still screaming, trying to break away from the police. At this point, Dave makes his way to the fire engine.

Dave asks, looking for his best friend, "Where's Bobby?"

The captain looks at the doorway filled with smoke.

"How the hell could you let him go in there?" Dave angrily asks, and then dashes to the sidewalk in front of the building, shouting Bobby's name over and over. "Bobby, Bobby, Bobby!"

Bobby is crawling up the stairs and in his mind he says, *I can hear you buddy.* He takes a deep breath and can hear the sound of his heart pounding. His mind echoes the statement to Kwamina the day before, *In my line of work, my life means nothing if someone's life is in danger. I just have to react and pray we both survive.*

Back outside, the crowd joins in chanting Bobby's name in cadence. "Bobby, Bobby, Bobby!"

The news crew maneuvers through the crowd to get to the captain for more coverage. "Captain Bonner, who is Bobby and why are they shouting his name?"

"He's the operator on my company and he is attempting the rescue of what we believe to be a little girl in a third story apartment. In case he becomes disoriented, the sound will help him establish a possible escape route."

"Thank you Captain," she says, as she adjusts her earpiece, "Thanks Phil. Connie Anderson, live at 104th St. and Lexington Ave. Firemen are trying to get a three-alarm apartment fire under control. The fire broke out shortly after 9:00. A five-year-old girl is believed to be trapped inside an apartment on the third floor. We're told a fireman is inside the burning building trying to locate the little girl. The girl's mother is said to be with police awaiting some word about her child. Of course, one can only imagine what she must be going through at this time, not knowing the fate of her child. Now, we're told that the child was home with her baby sitter when the fire started. The sitter managed to escape with her two siblings. We haven't had a chance to talk with the mother yet because authorities are telling everyone to stay back until they get the blaze under control. Again, a five-year-old little girl is said to be trapped inside this burning apartment building. Now all we can do is keep our fingers crossed with hopes that she will survive. That is the very latest from his scene. Of course as this story develops, we'll be back to update you. For now, Connie Anderson reporting live from the scene of a three-alarm apartment fire in the two-hundred block of 104th street. Back to you Phil."

"Connie, what is that chanting we're hearing in the background?"

Holding her earpiece she replies, "Captain Bonner explained to me that the chanting helps the fireman keep his bearings in the smoke filled building."

"Thank you Connie. Let's hope for the best. We'll give you live updates as we receive them. Now, back to your scheduled programming."

Bobby pushes open the door that he believes to be apartment 301. He removes his oxygen mask and shouts, "Little girl, where are you? I'm here to help you!" He can hear the chanting outside. He crawls around. In his mind he says, *Lord, if this little girl is here, please spare her life; this could be my little Sula.* He starts to back out, when miraculously, the smoke clears in front of him just enough for him to see what appears to be a clump of clothing on the floor by the window. He crawls toward the clump of clothes, moves it with his hand, and to his surprise, it's the little girl's lifeless body. Bobby attempts to shake her to conscientiousness, but she doesn't respond. He removes his oxygen mask once again, and gives the little girl two quick breaths. She coughs and starts crying. He places his mask over her face, scoops her up in his arms, and hugs her. "Everything is going to be alright. Let's go find mommy!"

Standing, he realizes the bottom floor is fully involved. There is no escape that way. He uses his oxygen tank as a battering ram as he shields the little girl with his fire coat to the best of his ability. In a swift backing motion, he breaks through a balcony door. The loud crash gets everyone's attention on the ground. The crowd realizes he has the child in his arms and roars with cheers. The mother falls to her knees, thanking God.

Fire Captain Bonner demands, "Get that ladder company through the crowd. We need it here now!"

At this moment, Dave frantically tries to make way for the ladder company when a fireman notices smoke being sucked back into the building. This is the first indication of the phenomena called "back draft." The fireman brings this to the captain's attention, and he gives orders, "Clear the area, clear the area; she's going to blow! Back draft!"

Bobby hears this and clearly realizes they only have seconds to get out of the building, or they will both die. The operator driving the ladder company continues to cautiously position his ladder truck to save his brother fireman and the little girl. The painful truth hits Bobby and Dave at the same time. There isn't enough time for the ladder company to get into position. There is a grim silence. Bobby and Dave look at each other. Dave removes his helmet; their eyes talk to each other. Bobby smiles and nods. Dave returns a reassuring nod, knowing his best friend's intentions. Bobby tosses the little girl outward so she can clear any obstacles and fall into Dave's outstretched, awaiting arms. The fall seems endless. Dave braces for the impact, catches her, and they both fall to the ground.

Two EMTs are there immediately with the captain. They remove the child from Dave's arms. One EMT assures everyone, "She seems to be fine."

Maritza runs to her daughter and embraces her, crying hysterically. Everyone looks toward the balcony where Bobby is helplessly standing. Dave gets to his feet and looks up just as the explosion occurs. Everyone is shielding themselves. Glass and debris fly everywhere. After the impact, Dave struggles to his feet once again. Everyone is beginning to stand.

The EMTs prepare to transport the little girl to the hospital. Dave looks up to where Bobby was standing, but he isn't there. Dave hears a scream and sees people pointing. Firemen are running in the direction of the pointing. It appears that the fire blew itself out and is no longer an imminent threat. Dave sees a body on the ground and realizes it could be Bobby. He rushes in that direction, pushing his way through the fireman. Falling to his knees, Dave pulls face up the lifeless body of his dearest friend. "Come on buddy, don't leave us damn it; don't die!"

In Bobby's dying breath, he gathers enough strength to pull Dave toward him and whispers in his ear.

Dave screams, "No, no!" as he frantically tries to resuscitate his lifelong friend.

The captain arrives with the EMTs; they check Bobby's vitals. They confirm to the captain with their eyes and a shake of their head that he's gone. Dave is determined to save him by administering CPR. The captain tries to stop him but needs help. Two firemen pick Dave up as he cries hysterically.

The chaplain asks curiously, "What did he say?"

Dave answers with a perplexed look on his face, "I'll see you in Paradise."

The chaplain gives Dave a reassuring nod with a hand on his shoulder. He then administers last rites. The news crew moves in and the reporter addresses the captain. "What can you tell me about this man?"

"Just what you witnessed; he is a hero. Don't release his name until his family has been properly notified." The captain looks at Dave, who is still being held up by the two firemen.

Dave acknowledges with a nod and says, "I'll go with the chaplain."

In the apartment, Vivianna is going about her daily chores. The doorbell sounds and Vivianna wipes her hands. Vivianna yells, "Coming!" When she opens the door, standing there, to her surprise, is a young man holding a beautiful bouquet of roses.

"Vivianna Washington?"

"That's me. They're gorgeous."

"They're for you."

"Why thank you," she says as she reaches for the roses. Vivianna takes the roses, locates the card, and closes the door. She slowly takes each step one-by-one as she reads the card. In Bobby's voice, the card reads, "Vivianna, the sound of your name delivers a bolt of rapture to my heart. The heavens are silenced, angels take notice, and birds take flight. You are my queen, the true love of my life, my driving force, and the mother of my three beautiful children. How could I forget? Fifteen blessed years of reciprocating love. Happy Anniversary my love! P.S. to prove Dave didn't remind me, there is a gift in the back of our closet; it's been there for weeks. Do not open until I return." As she reaches the top of the stairs, Vivianna smells the roses and clutches them to her chest. "I love you so much Bobby Washington, but you play too much!"

Vivianna pushes the front door open, runs into the bedroom, places the roses on the bed, and opens the closet door. She pushes the clothes aside and sees the beautifully wrapped gift on the floor in back. Vivianna pulls it out of the closet, shaking it softly, while listening and checking the weight. All the while she is wondering what could be inside. Vivianna walks out the room and places the box on the coffee table in the living room.

Back at the firehouse, as the units pull in, Jeremiah runs over to Bobby's unit. He notices Bobby is not driving and scans over the unit, jumping up and down. Kevin then approaches Jeremiah, plants his hands firmly on his shoulders, and delivers the bad news. Jeremiah sinks to his knees with his head clenched in his hands. He is in a state of disbelief.

When the doorbell sounds again, Vivianna hears the kids running up the stairs. The kids immediately notice her entire demeanor has changed for the better.

Kissing her children she says, "Hi my little darlings. Take off your church clothes."

Kwamina asks, "What happened while we were gone?"

"Your dad...that rat! He didn't forget our anniversary after all."

"I knew," Kwamina admits, as he smiles broadly.

"My first born—where is your loyalty to your mother?"

Rolling his fingers, Kwamina replies, "My loyalty has a price!"

"He paid you!"

"Nah."

Vivianna snaps at his buttocks with the kitchen towel. Kwamina goes to his room, passing the television, but the sound is muted. The fire captain is being interviewed.

Vivianna skips into the kitchen and pulls a pie out of the oven, burning her hand. Sucking her finger, she yells, "Ouch!" The doorbell sounds yet again.

Vivianna stops fumbling with the pie and thinks, *What, more gifts?*

Kwamina says, "I'll get it."

Vivianna insists, "Oh no, I'll get it. I'll bet that's for me." She takes her apron off and hurries down the stairs. Vivianna swings the door open with a broad smile, then freezes, not believing the sight before her eyes. She scans back and forth in disbelief. She falls back, grabbing her chest. Her mind flashes back to the fire on the television, the watchman saying, "He should be back in a couple of hours," and the note that read, "don't open until I return," all in their prospective voices. She immediately dismisses any negative thoughts. In a broken, trembling voice, she asks, "What's wrong?"

Dave can't answer; tears begin to stream down his face. The chaplain moves in toward her to comfort her, but she resists his advances.

Vivianna backs up while shaking her head in denial. "No, no, no. This is not happening to me!"

Dave cries, "Vivianna—"

"God, don't do this to me! Nooooo!" She falls to her knees and Dave falls with her, embracing her.

When the kids hear the commotion, Sula and Hakeem rush to the apartment door to see their mom on her knees crying. They cry in unison, "Mama…Mama!"

The chaplain rushes up the stairs to intercept their advances and brings them inside.

Sula wonders, "Where's my daddy?"

"Your father is in heaven with God," says the chaplain.

"Please ask God to let him come home," Sula pleads.

Hakeem cries, "I want my daddy. I want my daddy."

The chaplain embraces them both. Kwamina is standing in his room, refusing to come out to face the inevitable. He has a blank stare on his face and can hear his father's statement in his head, *Son, in my line of work my life means nothing if someone's life is in danger. I just have to react and pray we both survive.* Kwamina grabs his football off the bed and tosses it in the air—once, twice, and on the third time, he embraces it. With tears in his eyes he mumbles, "Dad, hold me. Dad, please hold me. And it's alright to kiss me."

Two weeks later, at the firehouse, Fire Captain Bonner says, "Dave, somebody's got to clear his locker."

"No captain, I can't do it."

"Dave, you know he would want you to do it."

Dave walks into the locker room and slowly approaches Bobby's locker. He puts his hand on the locker and pauses with his head down. Dave slowly opens the locker and reads Bobby's favorite scripture, Genesis 3:15, with a caption underneath that states "The victory is won!" He then looks at a picture of the family, then a picture of them in Nam, showing Bobby doing his favorite thing—giving him a headlock noogie. Reminiscing, he laughs. He also sees the "Fireman of the Year Award" from 1989. In his mind he thinks, *I think J would appreciate this.*

CHAPTER 3

Kwamina Falls in Love

Four years have passed since Bobby died. Kwamina is on his way to school. The scene is a busy New York street with pedestrians hustling to work.

A passerby notices Kwamina. "Hey Kwam."

"Hey what's up?"

As Kwamina bounces down the stairs toward the subway platform, he notices a beautiful young girl being harassed by three thugs. Passersby's notice her distress but refuse to help. Everyone ignores the situation, fearing the wrath of these thugs. Kwamina slows down, assessing the situation. He then comes to the conclusion that this girl doesn't know these guys and is terrified of them. Kwamina also knows by the girl's uniform that she attends Dominican Academy, an exclusive private all girls' school. A requirement of this prestigious school is that the students speak two foreign languages. Kwamina takes a chance and speaks to her in French in hopes of baffling the thugs and rescuing her at the same time. *"Pardonnez-moi, mademoiselle. Puis-Je vous rendre assistance?"* (Pardon me young lady, may I be of some assistance?)

"Oui, cher monsier. Je ne connais pas ces gens et j'ai peur." (Yes kind sir. I don't know these people and I'm afraid.)

Kwamina looks all the thugs straight in their eyes and moves in toward the girl. *"Excusez-moi, s'il vous plait les idiots! Votre haleine sens l'or tarni. En plus vous n'avez mem pas un joli mot et vou savez pas vous presenter! Allez, allezvous en stupides!"* (Excuse me please you idiots. Your breath smells like tarnished gold. Furthermore, if you have a decent wrap, you don't have a decent presentation! Now move out of my way stupids!)

The thugs, confused and puzzled, look at each other, shrugging their shoulders and shaking their heads.

"I knew she didn't understand anything. She ain't even American," says one of the thugs.

Kwamina diverts his attention back to the girl, *"Prenez ma main, madame, et sorton de ce fracas."* (Take my hand Madame, and Let's get out of this mess.)

Tiffany reaches for Kwamina's hand, when one of the thugs grabs her wrist in mid air. One of the other thugs points his finger in Kwamina's face as if pretending to hold a gun, while the third thug makes a loud sound. "Pow!"

The second thug pulls his business card from his pocket and addresses Kwamina. "Yo, teach her American and have her call me." Kwamina reaches for the card. He then grabs the girl's hand and pulls her out of the circle of terror. The two quickly walk away arm in arm.

Very hurriedly, she speaks in English, "Keep moving, don't look back. Are they following us?"

"Yeah, they're coming, run!" They take off running. When she realizes he was lying, she stops to catch her breath. Kwamina runs back to where she is.

Involuntarily hugging Kwamina, she says, "*Merci*...Thanks."

The two make eye contact. Kwamina pats her on her back reassuringly. "Is it gonna be English or French that we speak?"

"Let's stick to English cuz my French isn't as good as yours." They arrive at the subway platform. "How did you learn to speak French so well?"

"Well, my mom is third generation Creole from New Orleans. They speak French fluently and mom teaches us at home."

"What's Creole?"

"That's a history lesson I'll give you later."

"Excellent, your French is superb." Tiffany reaches for Kwamina's hand and introduces herself. "My name is Tiffany."

Kissing her hand, Kwamina answers, *"Je m'apelle Kwamina, mademoiselle."* (My name is Kwamina, young lady.)

"That's a beautiful name. Where did it originate?"

"It's Nigerian."

"But you're not African."

"No, but my mom thinks she is," he answers; they both laugh.

"You are so cool. That was very smooth what you did back there. It took courage and quick thinking, and I like that in my man." The subway pulls up to the platform.

"Dominican on East 68th right?"

"Yes, how do you know?"

Pointing at her uniform he says, "You're wearing your billboard."

"Oh, boy."

Boarding the subway, Kwamina says, "Let's go."

The passengers rush off the subway as others push their way on, hoping to find a seat. Kwamina finds two seats together on a row configuration. Kwamina and Tiffany sit together. An old woman appears and can't find a seat. Kwamina offers her his seat; she graciously accepts. As the subway pulls off, Kwamina notices another old woman in need of a seat. Kwamina looks at the young couple sitting next to them. "Hey man, would you mind giving your seat to this kind lady?"

The young man ignores Kwamina.

"Hey buddy, do you mind?" Kwamina asks again, then gestures to the old woman as Tiffany looks on. The guy looks away. "Oh, it's like that?"

The old woman hears Kwamina's plea and thanks him. "Son, it's okay; thanks for trying."

Kwamina stares the guy down with disgust. "He may be deaf and he's definitely dumb."

The fist old woman touches Tiffany's lap and speaks with admiration, "Your boyfriend is such a gentleman and handsome."

"That he is."

Kwamina hears Tiffany's answer and gives her a wink and a smile. Tiffany winks back, smiling.

Kwamina then turns his attention back to the rude guy, still seated. He becomes frustrated at this point and can't resist embarrassing him. In a loud voice he says, "You know, most people sit on their ass hole, but this poor girl has her asshole sitting next to her."

Everyone laughs, which embarrasses the guy and his girlfriend to the point that she takes his arm from around her shoulders so as to disassociate herself from him.

As the subway approaches Kwamina's stop, Tiffany wants to know, "How can I thank you for today, Kwamina?"

"We'll think of something."

"Call me tonight." They fumble, looking for something to write on, but realize the subway is stopping. Tiffany looks at Kwamina and he offers his forearm for her to write on.

"Go ahead; it's okay. Now I'll have to bathe tonight for sure."

As Tiffany writes her name and number, Kwamina pulls the thug's card out of his pocket with his free arm. "Hey, by the way, don't forget to call your new boyfriend, Master Funk Monkey," he jokes, as he hands her the card.

"Yeah right," she replies, as she tosses the card over her shoulder.

The subway comes to a complete stop. Kwamina notices the large writing on his arm. As he exits the subway he says, "Geez, I do have 20/20 vision you know."

Tiffany looks Kwamina up and down, "Yeah, so do I," she says in a sultry voice.

Kwamina arrives home from school. Walking towards his bedroom, he calls out for his mom. "Mom... Mom!" After throwing his books on the bed, he meets his mom in the living room.

"What Son...what?"

"Mom, I met the most amazing girl today. She is incredibly beautiful, she speaks French, and is she very smart. She kinda reminds me of you."

"I'm happy for you, Son. What's her name?"

"Tiffany Kendall," Kwamina replies as he pulls up his sleeve to reveal Tiffany's message.

Vivianna shakes her head at the startling sight of the large message on Kwamina's forearm. "Oh, that's a pretty name. I haven't seen you this excited since days with your dad." At the mention of dad, they both solemnly stare at the gift that is still on the coffee table.

Weeks later, as their relationship progresses, Tiffany and Kwamina spend as much free time together as possible. Tiffany and Kwamina are ice skating. He has never been ice skating before and has a difficult time gaining his balance. He encourages Tiffany to go on as she displays her skating prowess.

Tiffany and Kwamina are watching an emotional movie, *Sleepless in Seattle*, one evening. What's showing is the scene where Tom Hanks finds his son on the Empire State Building; this strikes an emotional chord with Kwamina. Tiffany is crying her eyes out and Kwamina is tearing up. Tiffany looks over at Kwamina and he turns his head away as if something catches his attention. He is clearly crying, but is embarrassed for Tiffany to see him. Tiffany leans forward and pulls his face toward hers and he resists, brushing her hand away. Tiffany wants to witness his emotion and throws popcorn in his face. They embrace laughing, while she still attempts to see his tear filled eyes.

That night, Kwamina is lying in his bed staring at the ceiling, while thinking about his newfound love.

Sula and Hakeem are on the sofa watching television. Vivianna is leaving her bedroom as the telephone rings. She looks toward Kwamina's room and dashes for the telephone. Kwamina hears the telephone and hurdles over the sofa, only to arrive a few seconds after Vivianna. Sula and Hakeem look on in amazement at their brother's agility. After Vivianna answers the telephone, she announces, "It's Tiffany."

Kwamina reaches for the receiver as Vivianna clutches it to her chest. He wrestles her for the receiver and tickles her until she releases it. With a broad smile, he answers the phone. Vivianna gestures that he is in love.

One warm day, Kwamina and Tiffany are walking in a park. Kwamina seats Tiffany and says, "You stay here." He runs over a small hill and neatly arranges a bouquet of flowers for her. He runs back over the hill and presents them to her on one knee. She grabs her mouth in surprise and accepts the flowers, "Oh my gosh, they're beautiful!" Tiffany leans forward and gives him a hug as they rock each other. They release as Tiffany strokes Kwamina's face. Tiffany gives Kwamina a longing look.

One afternoon, the couple promenades down 5th Avenue when Tiffany brings Kwamina's attention to Tiffany's Jewelry Store. She points to it and then strikes a pose in front of the store with the name of the store in plain view. Kwamina then pretends to be a photographer. He positions himself to take her picture with his make believe camera, but has to wait for passersby's to clear his path. He finally snaps his imaginary picture. They run to each other's arms, laughing and hugging. The embraced couple continues their walk when a large truck passes by, shaking the ground. In the foreground is a mother window- shopping, when a lovely dress catches her eye. She diverts her attention to the dress, releasing her baby's stroller unconsciously. Then suddenly, the stroller starts to roll toward the busy street. A group of teenagers, who are in a convertible, blaring their music and not paying attention, come speeding down the street. They speed up, trying to clear the caution light at the intersection. Kwamina notices the imminent danger of the stroller rolling in the path of the speeding vehicle. He abruptly breaks away from Tiffany, spinning her to the ground. She is bewildered and notices Kwamina grabbing the handle of the baby stroller. The mother, unaware of the scenario unfolding behind her, spins around to see Kwamina's hands on the stroller; realizing it wasn't where she had left it. Assuming an attempted kidnapping, she rushes to her child's spurious rescue, pummeling Kwamina with her purse and screaming, "Help, help! Onlookers witnessing the entire scenario are confused. Kwamina holds firmly onto the stroller, trying to shield himself from her blows with his free hand. Tiffany immediately gets up and runs to his rescue. She protects Kwamina while explaining to the woman, "No, no, what just happened was he saved your child's life." Figuring it out and noticing no one has come to her rescue, immediately the mother's entire demeanor changes. "Please forgive me, I owe you a debt of gratitude," she says, holding her chest and patting Kwamina's shoulders in apology. She checks on her baby while Kwamina pulls the stroller back. He then releases the stroller to the mother's care. Tiffany hugs him and pats his back. Kwamina is embarrassed by the attention as onlookers applaud. Dismissing the praise, the couple proceeds to cross the street.

As Kwamina and Tiffany enter Central Park, Kwamina spots a hot dog vendor and rubs his stomach, "I'm hungry what about you? One of New York's finest?"

Tiffany agrees, "Yeah, why not." He purchases their hot dogs and they walk away.

Kwamina offers Tiffany a bite, "Taste mine." She reciprocates the gesture and suddenly smashes her hot dog in his face and takes off running.

Kwamina stands in disbelief for a moment, then pursues her. He catches up to her and they both fall to the ground, laughing. As he looms over her, she notices he has chili all over his face and is hysterical. She wipes the chili from his face and licks her fingers as a sudden rush of intimacy overcomes them. Everything stops as they peer deep into each other's eyes. The moment has arrived and Kwamina moves in for their first kiss.

"Kwamie, I think it's time you meet my parents."

Sighing, he replies, "I agree."

Kwamina reaches his house and runs upstairs excitedly, bursting through the door. Sula feels his excitement. Not knowing what it's about, she joins him by jumping in place.

"Mom! Mom!"

Entering the room, Vivianna answers, "What, Son? Calm down," reaching for him.

Kwamina reaches for Sula, "Tonight is the night. It's got to be perfect."

Sula, with excitement, asks, "What, what?"

"At 7:00, I meet Tiffany's parents."

"That's all?" Sula says.

"Great! That's great!" Vivianna excitedly says.

"Mom, what will I wear?"

"Don't stress, I'll dress."

They give each other a high five. Kwamina walks into his room and goes through his underwear drawer. He holds up several pair, and to his dismay, he finds that they all have holes in them. "Hakeem, where's my pair of lucky drawers?"

Hakeem, who is in the living room, pulls his pants forward and pulls up the blue underwear Kwamina is looking for. "The blue ones?"

"Yes!"

"I have no idea," he answers and resumes watching television.

Kwamina, frustrated, selects the underwear with the least amount of holes and proceeds to get dressed. As his mom straightens his tie, she grabs him by his shoulders, peers at him square in the eyes, and advises him, "Remember, be the man your father taught you to be and you'll be fine, I know."

Kwamina gives her a reassuring hug and leaves.

Kwamina verifies the address Tiffany gave him and checks his watch, only to realize he is fifteen minutes early. He walks past the house, checking his watch every couple of minutes; timing it to arrive promptly at 7:00 p.m. It is now 6:57 and Kwamina walks toward the house. He rings the bell at precisely 7:00 and is greeted by the maid. He immediately offers his hand in friendship. She is confused and hesitant because this is unusual ethics; no one has ever offered to shake her hand.

"Good evening ma'am. My name is Kwamina Washington and I'm here to see Tiffany." Kwamina waits for the maid to introduce herself. She does not, so he asks her name. "And your name?"

"I'm Janice thank you," she says shyly, still shaking his hand. "May I have your coat?" She assists him with removing his coat and gestures for him to enter.

Kwamina walks forward in awe at the grandeur of the house. The maid joins him as Dr. Kendall appears across the room. "Sir, may I present Master Kwamina Washington, calling on Ms. Tiffany."

Dr. Kendall approaches curiously, looking Kwamina up and down. He immediately notices Kwamina's off brand clothing. Kwamina extends his hand. Dr. Kendall bypasses him, walks to the front door, and opens it; looking up and down the street. "Son, where did you park? I have an enclosed garage in the back."

"Mr. Kendall sir—"

"It's Dr. Kendall," he interrupts with an air of arrogance.

"Begging your pardon Dr. Kendall. I arrived here on the NJT."

Dr. Kendall gives Kwamina a puzzled look.

"Oh uh, New Jersey Transit."

With hands behind his back, Dr. Kendall walks toward Kwamina and circles him, as if to inspect him. Janice is in the background shaking her head in disbelief.

Mrs. Kendall enters the room with a broad smile. She offers her hand and Kwamina immediately reaches for it; bringing it to his lips. *"Enchante madame. Je peut voir pour quoi que at fille est is belle."* (Honored to meet you madame. I see why your daughter is so beautiful.)

Mrs. Kendall blushes and says, "Oh, I haven't a clue what you just said but it sounded so beautiful. Tiffany is the French speaker here. I've heard so much about you Kwamina."

Before Kwamina can answer, Dr. Kendall clears his throat so as to interrupt the mutual admiration. He shoots his wife a perturbed look. "Dear, Kwamina arrived here on the train," he says sarcastically. Dr. Kendall then diverts his attention back to Kwamina. He arrogantly asks, "From where?"

"Sir, I live in Harlem, near the Marcus Garvey Park."

Dr. Kendall gives his wife yet another look. "Dear I need a moment alone with Kwamina."

"I'll check on Tiffany," she quickly replies, as she exits upstairs.

Dr. Kendall looks over his shoulder and gives Janice a nod; she quickly retreats to the kitchen. "Son, don't you feel out of place here?"

Confused, Kwamina says, "I'm sorry sir—"

Dr. Kendall cuts him short, "That you will be."

Feeling the pressure, Kwamina appears to be getting nervous.

"So, I heard how you and Tiffany met, and I do thank you for that. But if it's money you're after, that can be arranged; you'll have to exit my daughter's life permanently."

"Sir, I don't need your money." Stuttering he adds, "I love your daughter."

"Love? Boy, you don't know a thing about love," he replies in a loud obnoxious voice.

"Sir, I beg to differ."

"Son, you're a good little actor. You have my daughter fooled and now you're working on my wife, but you can't fool me. You see, I know the area you're from and I know your type." He shakes his head up and down. "Con artist—but you can't get past me."

Meanwhile, Janice is in the kitchen with her ear glued to the door, taking it all in.

Tiffany and her mom appear at the top of the stair landing. Tiffany bounces downstairs and quickly realizes the atmosphere is not a very pleasant one. She stops, taking slow steps while listening to her father insult and belittle Kwamina. Kwamina is standing with his head down; his hands are behind his back, respectfully taking the onslaught.

"What's your price boy?"

"Sir, what I feel for Tiffany is priceless."

Dr. Kendall folds his arms, steps back, gives Kwamina a look and gestures toward the phone. "OKAY, I get it. You wanna make a phone call to your con artist daddy to see what his price is? That is, if you know who he is."

Kwamina's demeanor instantly changes. He takes a deep breath, stands upright, squares his shoulders off, lifts his chin up with pride, and pounds his clenched fist into the palm of his hand with every statement. He firmly says, "Sir, you can attack me, you can attack my character, but don't you dare attack my parents, especially my deceased father! He was a man you could only wish to be."

Tiffany can't take it anymore and screams from the stairs. "Dad, what are you doing?"

Dr. Kendall dismisses her with his hand.

Tiffany looks up to her mom pleading with her hands. Mrs. Kendall hangs her head in shame. "Mom?!"

"My father was an honorable man," Kwamina says as his voice begins to tremble with emotion. "He was a man who undoubtedly loved God and his family; a decorated soldier who served his country in Vietnam, as well as sacrificing his life to save another. How dare you attack my dad," pointing his finger in Dr. Kendall's face.

Hearing the entire argument, Janice whispers to herself, "Yes!"

Dr. Kendall steps back in shock and is speechless. He gathers his thoughts and points to the door. "I think it's time for you to leave."

Janice immediately bursts through the kitchen door and briskly retrieves Kwamina's coat. Tiffany tries to run to Kwamina, but is restrained by Mrs. Kendall. Mrs. Kendall attempts to pull her upstairs.

Tiffany reluctantly obliges and turns, screaming at her father, crying, "How could you do this to me? I finally fall in love and you destroy it. I hate you! You're destroying my life!"

"No young lady, quite the contrary, I'm saving your life, consequently saving you from this trash."

Kwamina and Janice look on.

"Furthermore, I defy you to see this boy. If I have the slightest inclination you're seeing him, you're out! No BMW, no shopping spree in France, and you can pay your own college tuition. Now, can he give you this?"

Tiffany looks over her father at Kwamina, who is in shock and has a blank look on his face.

Kwamina promises, *"Mon amour, ce qui se passe ici est un cauchemar. Je te prom ce n'est pas la fin de notre histoire."* (My love, what is happening here today is a nightmare. This is not how our story will end. I promise you.)

"Je t'aime Kwamie. Tu le sais, mais je ne peux me le permett en c"e moment. Comprends-moi s'il te plait." (I love you Kwamie, you know I do, but I just can't afford to right now. Please understand.)

"No je ne comprend pas." (No, I don't understand.)

Tiffany covers her face in shame and runs to her room crying.

Janice assists Kwamina with his coat, looks around to make sure the room is clear, fixes his collar, and looks Kwamina in his eyes. "You're a good boy. Anyone can see that. You deserve better than this. In all my years working for this man, I have never seen anyone stand up to him the way you just did. Thank you. I'll never forget this day." After they embrace, Janice opens the door. As Kwamina exits, she pats him on his back, watches him walk down the stairs, and wipes the tears from her eyes.

Kwamina sits on the train, staring out the window with a blank look on his face. When, in his mind, he hears, "God's Grace" by Trinitee 5:7. Tears begin to stream down his face.

As Kwamina climbs the stairs in a melancholy cadence, Vivianna hears him from inside; she senses trouble. Removing Sula from her lap, Vivianna opens the front door and waits for Kwamina at the top of the landing with open arms. He falls into his mother's arms.

"Mom, how could love feel so good yet hurt so bad? Her dad, I hate him!"

"Son, remember, I prepared you for this years ago. I don't know what happened, but if she really loved you she would be here right now. All things for a reason. The only thing parents can do is raise their children with the virtues and morals it takes to know right from wrong."

"But Mama is it wrong for me to love her?"

"No son, love has no explanation; it answers to nothing but our hearts. Sometimes it comes all at once and sometimes with friends, it gradually creeps up on you; but, friends first!"

"Mama, I did it right with all respect, if you know what I mean. But what went wrong? I hurt so bad."

"That's life son," she sighs and hugs him tighter. "It takes both people involved to realize, or rather, recognize true love outside of all material things—soul mates, like your father and I are."

Kwamina looks up at his mom as she gazes away. "But Mama...daddy is dead."

They both walk inside the apartment.

"Yes son, of the flesh, but not in my heart. He is here now more than ever before."

Kwamina looks at the neatly wrapped gift on the coffee table. "Is that why you keep this gift enshrined?"

Vivianna fights back tears as she reflects on her deceased husband. "Yes son. In my own crazy way, that's a part of your father I keep alive in a physical sense. To open that gift brings closure to something I am not ready to face yet." Vivianna hears Bobby's voice in her head saying, 'Don't open until I return.'

The phone rings and interrupts her thoughts. Sula answers it. Kwamina anticipates a call from Tiffany.

"Mama, it's grandmere. It's not that hussy Tiffany—break my brother's heart," she pouts with anger.

"Girl, give me that phone," she quickly demands as she takes the phone from Sula. "Hi Mama, I'm in the middle of a crisis with Kwamina...his first broken heart," she pauses and listens to grandmere. "I'll tell him and I'll call you back." Vivianna hangs up the receiver and laughs. Kwamina smiles and gives his mother a puzzled looked. Vivianna then composes herself and gives him the message from his grandmother. "Grandmere says, 'Why you need some bamoochie?' Now let me get this right. She meant to say bimbo hoochie, but she said, 'why do you need a bamoochie when you have her?'"

The conversation gets serious again. "Now you see son, that's unconditional love. If Tiffany really understood a love like that she would be here or on the phone. Instead, she's allowing her parents to live her life for her. True, they gave her life through God—a beautiful gift—but again, parents shouldn't try to live life like that. Know when to back off and just take a position to advise, guide, and praise their children's achievements and support them when they make mistakes."

"Yeah, she's a material girl living in a material world," Sula says angrily.

Vivianna admonishes, "Sula mind your business!"

Sula gets up and walks away. Not realizing how angered she is, she speaks out, "Breaking my big brother's heart makes it my business. I'd like to kick her ass!"

Vivianna and Kwamina look at each other with their mouths open in surprise.

Sula has a look of panic on her face and in her eyes and says, "Oh, Mama, I'm sorry." She grabs her mouth in surprise.

They all laugh. Kwamina opens his arms and Sula enters. Kwamina gives her a big rocking hug and a kiss on her forehead. He then looks at this mom, smiles and nods, "Yes."

"Time will heal that broken heart; and remember, we're here for you. One day, oh yeah Son, one day when she's riding in her BMW, she'll look over at some stuffy boring person just like herself and realize what a mistake she made. She'll never get over you. Loving you is so easy because you're special. The kind of love you experienced here is out there Son; she's out there. Be still and let God do his work."

CHAPTER 4

Recovery

Six months later...it is 7:00 a.m. and Vivianna is preparing breakfast and packing lunch for the kids. Kwamina is awakened by his radio alarm as a song is cued by a local DJ, Kim Boutte, on 97.1 WQHT. "Good morning New York, Kim Boutte here. You are listening to the cool jams of Hot 97. We are gonna kick it off for all of you Shai people out there." She cues the song "Baby I'm Yours". "Hot 97 keeping the hits rollin' and what about your friends?" She cues another song, "What About Your Friends" by TLC.

As Kwamina gets out of his bed, a male's voice is heard coming from Vivianna's bedroom. "Vivianna, I don't want no runny ass eggs this time and make my bacon extra crispy. You heard me?"

"I got it, I got it."

Kwamina whispers, "Damn, I hate him." Kwamina resumes his morning routine by awaking his siblings and making sure they get ready for school. Kwamina walks over to Hakeem's bunk and notices he is smiling in his sleep and has an erection. In amazement, Kwamina wonders what Hakeem is dreaming. In his dream, Hakeem is walking down the street, looking under womens' dresses with a mirror taped to his shoe. Kwamina takes his pillow and slaps Hakeem's erection. Hakeem awakens screaming and grabbing his groin.

"Ouch!"

"Boy, get your butt in that bathroom."

Hakeem, embarrassed, runs to the bathroom. Sula is awakened by the commotion and runs over to feed her pet mouse. Sula needs to use the toilet, but Hakeem is using it while eating a candy bar. Sula runs to the bathroom and bangs on the door.

Dancing in place she moans, "I have to use it. Hurry, hurry."

"I'm gonna fix you," Hakeem whispers to himself.

"Vivianna keep those kids quiet. I'm trying to rest in here."

Hakeem hears the voice and says with a smirk, "Oh, and I'm gonna get you too." Hakeem takes some toilet paper and smears chocolate all over it. He opens the door and chases Sula around the house with it.

"Mama! Mama!"

Vivianna begs, "Kwam, please help me."

Kwamina comes to Sula's rescue and grabs Hakeem by the arm in disgust. Hakeem then licks the toilet paper.

"Ugh!" Kwamina yells in disgust.

Hakeem immediately produces the candy bar. "Gotcha!"

They both laugh and Sula dashes to the bathroom. The two brothers walk to their room. Kwamina's arm is around Hakeem's shoulder. The two plot to remove their mother's nemesis.

In a sly voice, Kwamina says, "We've got to get rid of him."

Hakeem reassuringly says, "Let me handle this," reaching for his World War II helmet.

"Yeah, okay, just don't kill him."

Sula returns to the room and Hakeem enters the bathroom to execute his plot. Hakeem dumps the mouthwash down the drain and replaces it with Aqua Velva after shave. He then goes to the kitchen and sneaks a bottle of cayenne pepper past his mother. Hakeem returns to the bathroom and dips the Preparation H applicator in the cayenne pepper. He returns to the bedroom, hangs his helmet in its place, and brushes his hands together with a mischievous look on his face.

Smiling broadly, Kwamina asks, "Okay, what?" as he pauses from combing Sula's hair.

"Don't use the mouthwash this morning, trust me. And don't get hemorrhoids any time soon, trust me."

Kwamina nervously raises his hands to his face, "Oh my God, as if brushing the toilet with his toothbrush wasn't enough! How about the time you substituted the syrup with motor oil?" He returns to detangling Sula's hair.

"Ouch, ouch!" Sula whines.

"I'm almost done. Be still."

Hakeem finds it very humorous that Sula's ponytails are noticeably uneven. "Your ponytails are uneven."

Kwamina gestures behind Sula's back "No."

"Kwam?"

"Now stand up, this is the style. Put your hands on your hips and strike a pose. Tilt your head slightly to the left. There, that's it! Oh girl, you look so fine; just like a model." Kwamina winks at Hakeem to join in.

"Oooh yeah, that's it, like a role model," he adds while he rolls his hips.

"Now just walk with attitude and strut your stuff little mama."

Sula starts walking around the room like a super model. At that moment, Coconut, her pet mouse, dashes across the living room floor into Vivianna's bedroom. They can hear feet stomping about erratically. "Get that damn rat out of here! I'm gonna kill him!" yells the male voice.

Hakeem calmly says, "Man, be cool; he's after that cheese on your feet."

Sula is in a state of panic. "Kwam, please don't let him kill Coconut."

"Open the door and let him out!" he screams as he pounds on the door. The door opens and Coconut runs into Kwamina's hands. The kids go to the dining room to eat breakfast as Vivianna walks past them into her bedroom with her companion's breakfast.

"Kwam, please let me take Coconut to school. He's gonna kill him, I know."

"Baby girl, you can't take him with you to school. I'll take him with me today—he'll be fine." The kids finish their breakfast. "Mom, we're leaving," Kwamina calls out.

Vivianna comes out of the room, hands the kids their individual lunches, and kisses and hugs them good-bye.

Just outside the building, Hakeem stops and looks at his watch. "He should be in the bathroom right about now." When, all of a sudden, a loud scream is heard from the bathroom.

Screaming and spitting the male yells, "Ugh!"

CHAPTER 5

Communal Family

The loud noise startles the pigeons and they take flight. The kids take off running up the street laughing. They stop to catch their breaths and notice Ms. Ola; they greet her in succession from youngest to oldest.

"Good morning Ms. Ola."

"Good morning Ms. Ola."

"Good morning Ms. Ola."

Ms. Ola, who is eighty percent blind, is startled. She spins around and her wig becomes dislodged, covering her face. She parts the wig over her thick glasses to answer what she believes to be three kids. Squinting, she answers, "My babies, good morning!"

Kwamina notices she is speaking to the garbage cans. Hakeem attempts to laugh, but Kwamina grabs his mouth. Sula stands with her head still tilted. She notices a small garbage can with a mop in it and realizes Ms. Ola is speaking to it. "Sula, who put a rinse in your hair? Your plaits are so beautiful," she compliments as she leans back, holding her stomach.

Sula runs and hides behind the garbage can. "Thank you Ms. Ola."

"Hakeem you gettin' tall and handsome by the day sugar," she remarks as she chuckles with her hand on her hip.

Hakeem doesn't want to answer so Kwamina slaps him on his back. "Really Ms. Ola?"

"Baby, Ms. Ola wouldn't tell you a word of a lie. Kwam, sugar, you losing weight?"

Very polite and studiously Kwamina replies, "No Ms. Ola, not that I know of."

"Boy I tell ya, that Bobby Washington made some fine children praise the Lord."

Kwamina says, "Have a good day Ms. Ola," as he pulls his siblings down the street.

Ms. Ola turns to enter what she believes to be her apartment. She ends up in Mr. Jessie's apartment instead. "Damn it Ola! You in the wrong apartment again! I'm half naked!"

"And I'm half blind...praise the Lord! Who in they right mind would want to see your old, black, naked ass?"

"Right mind? You ain't even got a left mind. I'd tell you to go to hell but you probably couldn't find the place!"

"Jessie, stop while you can still move you ole feeble fool."

As the kids turn the corner, Sula insists they make their usual stop by a homeless man. The man leans against a building and wears a long overcoat. He has thick unkempt hair and a long beard. The man has a blank stare on his face. Sula, as usual, opens her lunch box to give him her apple. He doesn't respond so she places the apple in his hand. Sula looks at Kwamina, then attempts to give him her sandwich.

"No Sula. What are you going to eat?" Kwamina asks.

"I'll be fine Kwam."

"Okay, just take mine."

"Mister, when are you going to tell me your name?"

Hakeem dismisses the man, "Ah, that's nobody."

"Oh, Mr. Nobody, Hey Mr. Nobody," she says as she places her sandwich in his lap. "Bye Mr. Nobody." As Sula stands to leave, she notices the man making eye contact; he winks at her. In amazement, she winks back and gives him a thumbs up.

Just up the street, Kwamina decides to stop at Nguyen's Grocery Store to replace Sula's donated apple. Kwamina picks a nice apple from the fruit stand and places it on the counter. *"Xin chao buoi sang Mr. Nguyen.* (Good morning Mr. Nguyen.) How much for the apple?"

In his heavy English accent, Mr. Nguyen replies, "Five cent for you Kwanama, just for you."

"No Mr. Nguyen, it's Kwamina, not Kwanama."

"Yeah, I say Kwanama," he quickly replies as he brushes Kwamina off with his hands.

"And how much for the beautiful girl?"

Nhu, flattered, hides her face, smiling.

"Xin em vui long lay anh lam chong?" (Will you marry me?)

"No, no Kwanama. You no marry my daughter. I like you, but not like that."

Kwamina then notices a boy loading up his pockets with candy. The boy makes an attempt to exit, but Kwamina grabs him by the collar, removes the candy from his pocket and places in on the counter.

Mr. Nguyen looks on in total surprise. Kwamina slaps the boy in the back of his head. "Get outta here."

The boy takes off running.

"See Kwanama, you goot boy. I like you. I like you."

"You see, I marry Nhu. We make you beautiful Afronamese grandchildren."

Mr. Nguyen gives Kwamina a bewildered look. "You take apple, you take apple."

After exiting the store, the children make their way to the elementary school, which is a block away.

Sula says, "Kwam, let me tell Coconut goodbye." Sula reaches in Kwamina's book bag and strokes Coconut. In a baby patronizing voice she says, "Bye my little Coconut." Sula leaves the compartment partially open so Coconut can catch some air. Hakeem rolls his eyes in disgust. Holding his sister's hand, the two enter the school building and Kwamina makes his way to his school.

Kwamina recognizes a familiar figure from the back who could only be sticky fingers, Smukie the thief. He observes Smukie stealing a bicycle. Smukie proceeds to ride the bike towards him as a little boy comes out of a store screaming. "My bike! My bike!"

Kwamina blocks Smukie's path and stops him. The little boy runs toward his bicycle and Smukie surrenders it without a fuss.

"Kwamina, man I been looking for you," he says as he pulls up a sleeve to display stolen goods. "And if you don't need a time piece, time for the store to open." Smukie opens his coat to reveal all his stolen goods, which includes a prosthetic hand.

Kwamina looks at Smukie in disbelief. "You stole someone's prosthetic hand?"

"No, no Kwam. It's not prosthetic man; it works and they weren't using it anyway. And look what I have in the warehouse." Smukie turns around, pulls a string on his lapel and exposes a mini television on his back. "Whatever you wanna give me Kwam. Whatever you wanna give me."

"I've got something to give you."

Smukie, surprised, waits for Kwamina to go into his book bag. Kwamina comes up with Coconut and pretends to put Coconut in Smukie's coat. Smukie screams with fear and takes off running; leaving a trail of stolen goods behind. Smukie proceeds to remove his coat and shake his legs, still looking for Coconut. Smukie pulls his pants down, exposing his tattered briefs. Kwamina has a good laugh and continues his journey.

Kwamina clears the street to allow a garbage truck to pass. It stops a few feet in front of him when he notices the garbage men on the back. The men are cat calling and whistling at a tawdry dressed hoochie strutting down the sidewalk. She is wearing boots up to her knees, hoochie mama shorts, and a halter-top that is halting nothing.

One of the garbage men asks, "Damn girl, where are you going looking like that?"

The street-walker relishes the attention she is receiving. The driver then makes his way to the back of the truck to have a better look. "Hey baby, can I come with you?"

The street-walker places her hands on her hips and has an incredible attitude. "Hell no! Not looking and smelling like that."

Before the men could return insults, Kwamina interrupts. "Hey fellas, you're giving her just what she wants. You're playing right into her hands."

The same garbage man admits, "You're right; who the hell does she think she is?"

"Just who you're making her believe she is; someone special, by giving her this attention. She doesn't even know who she is. She has obviously lost her sense of identity. Come on guys, really, look at her. At least you men have good honest jobs. And what's her job?"

The street-walker has an inquisitive look on her face. Speechless, she listens intensely. The garbage men look at each other and nod their heads.

Two garbage men say simultaneously, "You're right."

The driver adds, "I work hard for my money."

With attitude, she says, "Let me tell y'all something—"

Before she could say anything more, the three men make a screeching sound with the "talk to the hand" gesture; they all say "Urgh!"

One man says, "It's the she garbage smells; and she doesn't know what we look like under these jump suits."

The street-walker imagines what these men would look like in Chippendale's attire—muscular, well-groomed, handsome men. She is taken aback by this revelation.

Kwamina interrupts by telling the men to acknowledge a beautiful woman walking on the opposite sidewalk. Kwamina encourages them to greet the woman. Gesturing with his head he says, "Guys look at that woman; address her like gentlemen."

The garbage men, with their newfound pride, address the beautiful woman.

One says, "Good morning ma'am."

Another asks, "How are you today?"

The driver compliments, "Lovely dress."

The woman, surprised, stops and acknowledges the men. "Good morning, I'm fine. Thanks for the compliment. You gentlemen have a nice day."

Kwamina announces, "Now, that's a lady. She's not advertising anything. Can you imagine what she looks like under that dress?"

The men imagine the woman walking away in her undergarments.

The driver exclaims, "Damn!"

One of the garbage me yells, "Get out of here!"

The other, in a daze, adds, "The imagination is powerful."

"See guys, that's what I'm talking about—lady," pointing up the street, "hoochie," pointing at the street-walker. Laughing, Kwamina walks off and the garbage men pull off in their truck, blowing exhaust fumes in the street-walker's face.

As Kwamina makes his way to school, he notices his friend Paula, who has Down's syndrome. She has always had a crush on him. Paula is in the yard assisting her mother with yard work.

"Hi Mrs. McMurray."

"Well, hi Kwamina," she replies, as she ties the garbage bags.

"Let me get those. Paula, blue really works for you girl. You got it going on!"

Paula is blushing uncontrollably and says, "Oh Kwam, you say some nice things to me."

"And who was that guy I saw you with the other day?"

"Oh," she says, sucking her teeth, "he's just a friend."

"He better be cuz I'll make him just a corpse. Remember, you're my woman. Now give me a kiss so I can get to school."

Continuing his journey, Kwamina recognizes from behind a call girl named Leila. She is someone who has a special place in his heart. "Hey yo, Leila!"

Hearing her name, Leila turns around. Noticing who it is, she advances toward Kwamina with a broad smile and outstretched arms. They embrace in a big bear hug, rocking side to side. Patronizing him, she says, "Oh, my little crush."

"Oh Leila, I just can't give you this bruised heart; but when it heals, it's all yours."

"You are so smooth for your age," she compliments as they walk embraced, "the things you come up with. Umma start calling you dangerous. You always get my attention."

"Leila you get enough attention. Look across the street."

They both turn their attention to Uncle Boosie's Barber Shop where five patrons and Uncle Boosie are infatuated with Leila's breathtaking beauty. Old Man Ulysses is licking a slug trail on the glass. Boosie has an inviting look on his face. "Boy I'd like to tune her chello and slap that Jell-O."

One of the patrons has his lips hard pressed against the glass, while the second patron is flashing his money.

Stan stutters, "That's..." very clearly he adds, "a fine girl!"

Another patron screams, "Shut up! You can talk when you want to. Boy I'd sure like to butter those biscuits," licking his lips and adding, "that's one assy...I mean classy broad!"

Leila, completely embarrassed, says, "Oh my god!"

Kwamina shakes his head in shameful disbelief.

"So Kwam, how's school?"

"Four point o, can't do no mo. Leila, I read your last poem to my English Lit professor. He was impressed and he'd like to meet you!"

"Get outta here!"

"No Leila, he's tough as nails. And to impress him, huh, you are super gifted! It pains me to see you wasting this gift. You are so loveable and smart. I have to fight to keep from falling in love with you. Leila, what happened? Is it for the money?"

"I knew you'd ask me this one day. I feel you're old enough to understand now. Nah, the money has little value to me Kwam, maybe no value at all. All I have to show is a wardrobe of tantalizing outfits and a collection of shoes any woman would envy."

"You're being evasive. What's up?"

"My first love pimped me; he made me turn my first trick. Kwam, I thought he loved me; he told me he did. No one ever held me like he did. I never knew my father. Everything was fine until he had needs I didn't understand. We just didn't have the money. Then, one day, I realized I was supporting his drug habit. He physically and emotionally abused me. I was lucky to escape with my life."

"My point exactly—*your* life. You're not the person you've become. You're Satan's toy."

"Kwam, these men are faceless blurs who pay for satisfaction like it's a fantasy buffet. As soon as I'm done, I take long showers to scrub them off; I feel clean."

"But Leila, a little piece of you leaves with every man you're with. One day you'll be an empty shell with nothing left and I don't wanna witness that. Leila don't lose your soul. Back then is when you lost Leila. But I know she's here," he says as he touches her chest. "I'm going to help you find her and love her again. We need positive, righteous people in our lives. I'm going to help you matriculate into mainstream society. I'll do whatever it takes to get you back into school. Phone calls, paperwork—I'll even get a job to help you pay for it."

Obviously moved by the love and concern Kwamina shows her, tears begin to stream down Leila's face. Kwamina gives her a big hug.

Stroking Kwamina's face, she says, "Umma think about it. I'll give it some serious thought." Leila departs and Kwamina proceeds toward Uncle Boosie's Barber Shop.

One patron is receiving a hair cut from Boosie. Two more patrons wait to be serviced, while Stan and Old Man Ulysses play a game of checkers.

Old Man Ulysses asks curiously, "Boy, you tappin that?"

The man getting his hair cut laughs and says, "Kwamina can't afford that."

Boosie adds, "It ain't about a dollar it's about the motion," he clenches his fists and thrusts his hips.

Old Man Ulysses retorts, "I see she ain't motioned her ass over here to you yet."

Boosie dismisses the old man's insult. Stan makes an attempt to greet Kwamina. "Kw—"

Old Man Ulysses teases, "Hooked on phonics failed you. Shut up and play checkers you f...reakin idiot."

Again, Stan tries to speak to Kwamina. Stuttering badly, he says, "K—"

Kwamina instructs, "Now Stan, remember your exercises. What's happening is your brain is out thinking your tongue. Relax your throat as if you were yawning and feel the hypoglossus muscle tighten. Feel it," as he touches the base of his throat.

Stan does the exercise.

"Relax and tighten—now that could be an oxymoron."

Boosie mimics Kwamina and points at Old Man Ulysses with his comb. Jokingly, Boosie says, "And that could be a black moron."

Stan continues to do his exercises. Old Man Ulysses stands up and motions as if to unzip his pants. "Boy, watch how you doin that."

Stan stands with fists clenched while biting his bottom lip Ali style.

"The funny thing is, people who stammer have surprisingly strong tongues."

Boosie begins to stutter, "I...can believe that," flickering his tongue.

Stan, tricking Old Man Ulysses, looks over his shoulder and makes him believe he sees another fine woman. While looking outside, Stan exclaims, "Ooooh!" While Old Man Ulysses' attention is diverted, Stan rearranges the checker board to his advantage. Stan exchanges winks with Kwamina.

Another patron says, "Anybody can play checkers. It takes a man to play chess."

Old Man Ulysses brags, "Boy let me tell you something. I was a young boy playin' chest. Clementine, that girl had big ole country corn fed titties. When I played chest I didn't come up check mate, I came up with a mate and three children. I ain't playin' chess no more; umma stick to checkers."

Boosie adds, "When you ain't playin' checkers you playin' wit yourself."

"Yeah, self go right to work and never tell me no," Old Man Ulysses remarks as he makes a jerking motion with his hands.

Everyone laughs.

A different patron adds, "Your mind is a terrible thing, it's waste."

"You know why his mama named him Ulysses? Because she couldn't spell useless!" Boosie pipes up.

Again, everyone laughs.

While reading the newspaper, Old Man Ulysses says, "Another drive by. Huh…in my day, when you did a drive by you didn't take a life—you left one there nine months later."

Everyone laughs and gives the old man dap.

The man getting his hair cut says disgustingly, "That better be a clipper in your pocket," as he jerks his arm away from the chair.

Boosie asks slyly, "Just as hard, huh?"

"You disgust me! I don't know why I keep coming back here."

"Maybe to feel this clipper," he replies while gyrating on the chair arm. "What, you wanna leave now?" he asks while his patron has half a haircut. Boosie digs in his nose and looks for a spot to place his booger.

"Man, where you gonna put that?"

"I keep 'em close to me cuz I recycle them; good lil snacks," he says while putting the booger in his pocket.

"I don't know why I ask you."

In the background, Kwamina is brushing his hair.

Boosie inquires, "Hey boy, how is that fine mama of yours? I told you to give her my number."

"Oh, she's got your number."

"If I had sense enough, I'd think I'm being insulted. You kinda late today ain't you boy?"

"Oh no, umma tutor today."

"Umma tooter every day," Boosie replies as he expels gas.

"Ah man!" the patrons exclaim simultaneously, while fanning their faces.

"You don't like it, you can take your business somewhere else. Nappy head bastards always dulling up my clippers."

Kwamina says, "That's gross."

"Speaking of gross, meat spit, get your money out. I had pork chops this morning. Damn it I'm feelin' it today, double or nothin."

One of the waiting patrons asks, "Double or nothin?"

"Yeah you heard me." Everyone scrambles as Kwamina collects the bet. Boosie has a bull's eye drawn on his mirror with specks of dried meat trophies. Boosie begins to pick his teeth and sucks for a sizable piece of meat to spit at the bull's eye. Everyone encircles, awaiting anxiously. Boosie positions his head and licks his finger, checking wind direction. While clearing his throat he says, "According to Newton's first law of motion—"

Old Man Ulysses interrupts, "Newton? The only Newton you know is fig newton fool!"

"Begging your ignorant pardon. Velocity does not equal 0 m/s; acceleration does equal 0 m/s2."

Very impressed, Kwamina says, "Touché."

The man getting his hair cut says impatiently, "Come on already."

Another patron adds, "Man will you spit, this is my lunch money."

Boosie spits bull's eye and everyone is disappointed. "Uh, you'll be fasting today my man. Give it up."

Kwamina gives Boosie his winnings.

Boosie hands Kwamina $5. "Here, here—get outta here. There's your lunch money going out the door. Just goes to prove...can't beat my meat!"

Kwamina exits the barber shop and passes Maritza's Beauty Salon next door. His intentions are to wave and continue, but Maritza notices him and motions him in. Maritza employs three flaming gay guys, one of which is a cross dresser. Michaela and Jamie style hair, while Jamie's customer receives a pedicure from Alexa. Kwamina enters the salon and is greeted with open arms and a big hug.

Glad to see Kwamina, Maritza asks, "*Kwamina, como estas papi?*" (Kwamina, how are you?) Maritza releases Kwamina, steps back and looks him over. "You look good!"

The gay guys are talking in the background.

"Kwam, I see you talking to that girl," she says as she gestures across the street. "What's up with *su novia* (your girlfriend) Tiffany?"

"Doesn't look good."

"I'm sorry to hear that. Kwam, that life your dad saved is eating me out of house and home. I don't know if he did me a favor or not. *Ay que lindo!*" (Oh my goodness!) Maritza retreats to her desk and continues to do paperwork.

Michaela speaks in an exaggerated mockery of Maritza's accent, "Ju look good to me papi."

Alexa says with attitude, "Oh, I smell," while sniffing the air, "you just came from Testosterone Town."

Jamie asks, "Speaking of smell, Michaela what's that fragrance you're wearing?"

"Why Jamie, Chanel No. 5."

"Hum, smells more like WD No. 40," he retorts as he rolls his neck with his hands on his hips.

Alexa offers, "Girls, yall should try my Charlie."

Jamie replies, "Alexa honey girl, you can keep your Charlie. I'll find my own."

"Senoritas no cat fights, we have guests."

While looking at Kwamina's groin, Alexa asks, "Kwam, can I do something to—" He then looks up at Kwamina, "I mean for you?"

Michaela warns, "Watch it girl."

Alexa begs, "Somebody get me a phone book."

Jamie asks, "What you need a phone book for tramp?"

"Child I need to call a construction company for these feet. And you want a manicure too? Are you gonna lay anymore bricks today?"

"Alexa, *silencio*! Silence!"

"*Adios* Senora Maritza," Kwamina says as he prepares to leave.

"Hasta luego." (See you later.)

Michaela says, "Bye sexy."

Jamie adds, "Later baby."

With a sheepish look Alexa says, "I owe you a massage."

"Okay...bye guy...urls," Kwamina replies, as he turns to leave.

Just around the corner, Kwamina sees yet another familiar face.

Tony says, "Yo Kwam what's up?" as he throws his hands in the air, giving Kwamina a soul shake. A fine girl passes by and catches Tony's eye. While looking over his shades, Tony exclaims, "Ooh wee! Damn! Hey lil mama, the name is Tony and I'll be yo tiger. Grrrrr..."

Kwamina shakes his head and says, "More like Tony, the wanna be black. Yo Tony you've got so much to be proud of—your heritage bro." Kwamina then takes his index finger and underlines Tony's name as he says it, "Anthony Collatta, Italian. Famous Italians, heads up; Galileo, the first known astronomer; and you always wear Armani suits."

"Yeah."

"And remember Old Blue Eyes, Chairman of the Board?"

"Frankie, yeah."

"And Tony the Yog, Yogi Bear."

"Man yeah! Yo, Kwam, you forgot my main man Rocky Balboa, the Italian Stallion."

"That's what I'm talking about," he says as he offers Tony a high five. "Now that's your lesson for the day," he adds as he walks away.

"Hey Kwam, what's that first one? That Gigolo guy?"

"No, Galileo."

"Yeah, yeah, yeah!"

As Kwamina continues, he checks his watch, and methodically times his steps to arrive purposely at a certain gentleman's front door. Through routine, Kwamina knows that at a precise time every morning this gentleman comes out to retrieve his paper. We find out later this gentleman is Ron Hessler, a retired detective. Kwamina always greets him and is ignored. His wife, on the other hand, answers with a friendly wave. In his own whimsical way, Kwamina is determined to break this silence.

"Good morning, sir."

Kwamina is again ignored.

"Good morning, ma'am."

Mrs. Hessler says in a very friendly voice, "Good morning young man." She turns to address her husband, "That's a nice boy. Every morning he greets us. Don't be so uptight. Can't you loosen up?" She is ignored; her husband returns inside.

As Kwamina proceeds to school, he sees an older woman leaving her apartment, closing the gate behind her. Noticing she dropped what appeared to be an envelope, Kwamina picks it up; realizing it is full of money. As Kwamina runs toward the woman, her skinhead son sees this from their fourth floor apartment window. When Kwamina touches the woman on her shoulder, she spins around, clutching her purse; which appears to her son to be a mugging in progress. His immediate response is to come to his mother's defense.

Kwamina backs off with his hands up and says, "No, no ma'am; you dropped this," while handing the envelope to the woman.

Realizing she dropped the envelope with her rent money, she takes the envelope from Kwamina and clutches it to her chest. "Oh, son, thank you so much. Thank you!"

Kwamina nonchalantly dismisses the deed, "It's okay ma'am. Have a good day," as he walks away.

The woman's son reaches her, looking around for Kwamina. He then sees Kwamina up the street and yells, "I'll get that nigger!"

The woman grabs her son by the shirt, pleading with him. "No, no, look! It's the rent money. I dropped it and he returned it to me—it's all here."

Kwamina, hearing the commotion, turns around and sees the woman's son. The two make eye contact and her son gives a nod of approval. Kwamina returns the nod. Meanwhile, on the opposite side of the street, a group of fellow skinheads notice the commotion and anticipate trouble. Not understanding the scenario that played out before them, they pursue Kwamina without probable cause. Cognizant of the impending attack, Kwamina flees for his life, putting his agility to the test. Kwamina turns the corner and ducks in an alley in an attempt to elude his pursuers. Kwamina then notices Mama Rosa on her usual perch in her window. As the skinheads turn the corner, Mama Rosa shouts out while pointing in the opposite direction, "He went that way."

Kwamina emerges, bows his head, and throws a kiss to Mama Rosa. She smiles and returns his kiss. Kwamina reaches the subway station, passes through the turn style, and waits for his train. He then spots the skinheads coming down the steps; they notice him simultaneously. They hurdle over the turn style and run through the crowd towards Kwamina. As the train approaches, Kwamina runs toward the end of the platform, hoping to buy himself some time. The train comes to a stop. Commuters rush off as Kwamina rushes on. The skinheads finally arrive as the doors close in the nick of time. Kwamina, overcome with relief, jeers at the frustrated skinheads. He then drops his book bag and announces, "I happen to have your two newest members with your leader in the middle." He then moons the skinheads and presses his buttocks against the glass. The other passengers are hysterical with laughter. The train pulls off as the skinheads run alongside it, vowing to kill Kwamina. The first skinhead doesn't see a post and runs right into it, *ping*! Everyone laughs even louder. Kwamina notices the woman's skinhead son coming down the steps and opens his arms in a questionable gesture. The skinhead returns the gesture.

CHAPTER 6

An Unexpected Twist of Fate

In the lobby of a luxurious penthouse building on Park Ave. is where native New York aristocrat Loretta Marullo struggles with her dog Bruno. Noticed by Doug the doorman, he scurries to her aid. "Good morning Mrs. Marullo, where is Daisy?"

"Oh Doug she's running late and Bruno can't wait," she replies, as she is being pulled away by Bruno.

Arriving at the bus stop from the subway station, Kwamina looks for the bus down the street. Shielding himself from the wind, he backs up onto a perch hidden by some bushes. As she walks her dog, Mrs. Marullo and the bus approach at the same time. Kwamina leaps out, startling Mrs. Marullo. She is taken by surprise and grabs her chest. She falls backwards and Kwamina leans forward in an attempt to break her fall. The bus driver is frightened by the presumed mugging in progress, decides not to stop, and accelerates. Not able to maintain his balance, Kwamina and Mrs. Marullo fall to the ground. At that moment, two police officers a block away observe their fall; they watch in shock.

Officer Firmin says in shock, "What the hell?"

Looking in Firmin's direction, Officer Wilson says, "I can't believe this—in broad daylight."

"Let's get this stupid nigger."

In a panic, Kwamina says, "Ma'am I'm so sorry. Are you alright?"

With labored breaths, Mrs. Marullo replies, "My heart, intro."

"Where ma'am. Where is your intro?"

"In my, in my…" Mrs. Marullo goes limp.

As the officers speed toward the scene, Kwamina is going through Mrs. Marullo's mink and purse, trying to locate her medication.

Firmin calls the incident in, "203, 10-28."

The police dispatcher asks, "What you got?"

"Possible robbery in progress on Park and 51st."

"All units clear the air until I get a code four from 203."

"We have a black male between eighteen to twenty, wearing blue jeans, brown jacket, and a back pack. He has an elderly white female down and he's going through her purse."

Realizing she is fading away fast, Kwamina checks Mrs. Marullo's vitals. Feeling her carotid artery, Kwamina realizes her heart is in fibrillation; he administers the pericardial thumb and CPR.

The officers arrive. Officer Firmin restrains Kwamina by positioning his billy club under Kwamina's chin. Confused, Kwamina resists. Firmin yells, "Wilson, he's going for my gun!" Officer Wilson immediately draws his weapon. As he cocks the gun, Bruno attacks. He gets a shot off, striking Kwamina in the buttocks. Kwamina gets to his feet and makes his escape, limping. While fleeing, he is caught on camera by a tourist.

Wilson is distracted by Bruno's attack; Firmin runs to his aid. Bruno retreats and licks Mrs. Marullo's face.

The incident is called in by Firmin, as Wilson checks his injuries. "203, shots fired, officer down. My partner is possibly injured. Perpetrator fleeing north on Park, possibly hit. Be advised, we have an elderly white female on the sidewalk unconscious.

The emergency unit arrives and the EMTs immediately rush to Mrs. Marullo's assistance. Bruno still stands guard over his beloved owner. Sensing no threat, he yields to the EMTs.

"Move dog, move," yells one of the EMTs.

The other says, "Get outta here."

Bruno then retreats while the EMTs check Mrs. Marullo's vitals.

"Doesn't look good," the first EMT says, as he prepares Mrs. Marullo for transport.

"Undoubtedly, CPR would've helped."

Bruno observes as his owner is being hoisted into the emergency unit. As it speeds away, he follows. At a busy intersection, the ambulance makes its way through pedestrians and traffic. Bruno is cut off by pedestrians who are eager to make it to their destinations. Bruno loses the ambulance. Confused, he picks up Kwamina's scent and attempts to locate him.

Limping, Kwamina discovers an abandoned warehouse and enters through a small crawl hole. While addressing his wound, Kwamina is surprised by Bruno's presence. "Get outta here. Go, go!" he demands, while snapping and brushing Bruno away.

Bruno whimpers and reluctantly leaves.

The Kendall's are tuned in to the news. Tiffany is in complete shock.

The news anchor reports, "An affluent aristocrat, Loretta Marullo, was mugged and believed to have been murdered this morning on the corner of Park and 51st. The suspect, Kwamina Washington," as his picture is being shown, "was wounded at the scene and escaped. The suspect is at large and the incident is currently under investigation."

Dr. Kendall smirks and says, "Huh, I told you so."

The Mayor announces, "I knew Mrs. Marullo personally and I vow to prosecute this boy—"

A reporter interrupts, "Mr. Mayor isn't he a suspect at this point?"

"...this suspect to the highest extent of the law. I will work closely with the DA's office and I promise, justice will be served!" He looks directly into the camera and says, "And remember, this is a capital punishment state." The mayor walks off, followed by his assistant. "Mrs. Marullo was a major contributor to my campaign. There has to be a conviction. Get on the phone with the DA. When they find this boy, make sure he doesn't make bail. If I'm going to be re-elected we have to lean towards the death penalty. He owes me one and I want this one. I'll have this election in the bag."

At the community meeting Vivianna announces, "I would like to thank everyone for showing us your love and support. As we all know, my son is not capable of committing such a heinous crime. So, let's get right to business. This meeting is closed to all law enforcement personnel, but open to the media. I know my son is out there suffering, as well as the Marullo family. At this moment, we'd like to acknowledge them by having a moment of silence. Everyone is silent for a few moments.

"However, I am determined to prove my son's innocence. The first thing on my agenda is an attorney. The fire boot is being passed around for donations to retain an attorney for Kwamina's defense. Any suggestions?"

"Johnny Cochran?" came a voice from the crowd.

Everyone laughs.

"We can't afford him."

Dave, who is passing the boot, stops and raises his hand for acknowledgement.

"Yes Dave. Go ahead."

"What about Paul Goldberg?"

Some in the crowd laugh while others gasp, but they all disapprove. Vivianna gives Dave a puzzled look.

Someone says with disgust, "He's a drunk."

Another person pipes up, "We can dry him out and clean him up."

Dave walks toward the podium. "Yes, that he is. But he was the best defense attorney in the city. He is a victim of his circumstance, but he still has the ability. He hasn't practiced in a while, but I think I can resurrect him. Vivianna, I have a gut feeling about this man. I'm pretty persuasive, so let me handle this."

Vivianna sighs and gives in, "Okay, Dave."

At that moment, Jeremiah walks in.

A person in the crowd announces, "Hey everybody look! It's Jeremiah Duplesis, Giants Probo QB!"

The crowd is extremely complimentary and mobs Jeremiah.

Vivianna says, "Everyone, please let him through."

Jeremiah advances to the podium where Vivianna meets him with open arms. "Hi Mrs. Washington.

I saw the news and I got here as soon as I could. I have something for you." Jeremiah reaches in his coat pocket and hands Vivianna a check for $15,000. Vivianna accepts the check with gratitude, holding it to her chest.

"Thank you Jeremiah. Oh thank you."

"No, thank you, Mrs. Washington. Had it not been for this family, especially Mr. Bobby, I wouldn't be the person I am today. I adopted him as my father for all of twenty-seven hours and I feel like he gave me twenty-seven years of love. He believed in me when no one else did and encouraged me when no one else would. It was on his advice that I tried out for the team. Now, here I am. I owe it to you. Thank you." The moment Jeremiah steps down he is mobbed again.

"Order, order everyone. Next on our agenda, we need to find Kwamina and have him turn himself in. Does anyone have any idea where he is?"

Smukie enters his den through his crawl hole to store his latest booty. He notices a trail of blood and recalls his friend. Kwamina is wounded and still at large. Playfully, Smukie tastes the blood. "Um...tastes like chicken. Gotta be a brother. Kwam, you in here, dog? You got thirty minutes. Umma watch the ten o'clock news and if they offer a reward umma turn yo black ass in. Alright, time is ticking," he yells as he turns to leave.

"You alone?" Kwamina asks, as he emerges from the shadows.

"Man where they shot you? They tryin' to throw a murder charge on you. Man, I been tryin' to get shot! You ain't no real man until you been shot. Let me see, let me see."

"Man, can the dumb shit! They're gonna kill me; I know it.

We gotta figure something out," he says as he grimaces in pain.

"Man I know the sewer system."

"No man. I gotta turn myself in. I'm innocent."

"Man, your peeps are meeting at St. Ignatius right now, but they wouldn't let me in."

"Smuk, go back and get my mom. No police, just my mom."

Smukie surveys his warehouse of stolen goods and gives Kwamina a look. "Duh? You sure no police? They're not gonna let me in anyway."

"Yeah they will. Get word to my mom and tell her to be *an exception to the rule*. That'll get you in."

"Okay dog, I got your back. Man, we need to get you to a hospital."

Grimacing, Kwamina mutters, "Smuk, hurry up man. I'm losing a lot of blood."

Smukie arrives at the St. Ignatius Center door, which is being guarded. The guard tells Smukie in a demanding voice, "Told you once to get out of here. Now stop bothering us."

"Man I ain't here for that. I need you to get a message to Mrs. Washington that is of the most urgent nature."

"What fool?"

"Just tell her to be an exception to the rule and she'll understand. It's like a top secret code you idiot!"

The guard gives Smukie a questioning look and pulls a bystander. "Watch this door for me, and don't let this fool in. And remember, no police."

The guard walks through the church center crowd and whispers the message in Vivianna's ear. She nods "yes" and the man gestures to allow Smukie's entrance. Smukie enters and washes himself with holy water, as he is noticed by everyone. They immediately check their valuables. Smukie walks toward the podium and passes the guard with a patronizing smirk. The guard casually checks for his wallet and notices it's missing. He collars Smukie and pulls him back. Smukie reaches into his coat and in one motion, hands the guard his wallet.

"Count it; it's all there—all $3. You need to use two of them to buy some breath mints," he says under his breath, while waving his hand in front of his nose.

With fists clenched, the guard advances toward Smukie. Smukie scurries toward Vivianna. Proudly he announces, "I know where Kwamina is."

The crowd gasps in disbelief.

"He wants just you Mrs. Washington," he says as he looks around, "and no police."

The crowd follows Vivianna and Smukie. The news media has tipped off the police to Kwamina's presumed hiding place. As a result, a SWAT team has been dispatched. As they arrive at the warehouse, Smukie is cautious to keep his secret entrance concealed. "Mrs. Washington, stay here. I'm going to open the big door."

Smukie enters the warehouse and calls out for Kwamina. "Kwam, I'm here with your mom and about fifty other people—but no police." At that moment, sirens are heard and blue and red lights are reflecting. "Geez, I didn't bring em! Come on man, your mom is outside. They ain't gonna do nothin."

Kwamina emerges from the shadows and mumbles, "Bring mom in."

Smukie opens the door, walks outside, and realizes thirty rifles are trained on him. As they lock and load, he dives to the ground with his arms outstretched. Vivianna runs to his aid and shields his body with hers.

"Come on, Son."

"Oh no, Mrs. Washington. These trigger happy fools will kill me dead."

Vivianna yells, "Don't shoot! Don't shoot! This is not my son."

The police captain orders his men to stand down. Smukie slowly and cautiously stands up. "Ma'am come this way. We have the building surrounded. Please let us do our job."

"No, he is my son and I'll bring him out myself." Vivianna and Smukie enter the warehouse as the news crews frantically prepare for a live report. "Son, come to me. It's gonna be okay, I'm here."

Kwamina comes out of the shadows and Vivianna dashes to him.

"Mom, I didn't do it."

"I know son. I know. Where are you hurt?"

"My leg."

"We need to get you some medical attention. It's gonna be okay baby. Come on." With one arm around his mother's neck, and the other around Smukie's neck, they assist him as Kwamina hobbles toward the door.

Smukie yells, "We're coming out and we're not armed!" Vivianna and Kwamina look at Smukie in disbelief.

Smukie admits, "Sounds good—it works in the movies," shrugging his shoulders. As the three exit the warehouse, the police rush and subdue Kwamina.

The day after the community meeting, Hakeem does an outstanding job of passing out flyers. He is down to one flyer and is extremely exhausted. As he turns the corner, he sees Mr. Nobody in his usual spot.

Hakeem mumbles to himself and sighs, "I'll probably waste this last one on Mr. Nobody, but at least I can honestly say I handed them all out." Hakeem drops to the ground next to Mr. Nobody, with his head on Mr. Nobody's arm. "Here Mr. Nobody," dropping the flyer on his lap. "Not that you can read this. It's about my brother who is being accused of a murder he didn't commit. Kwam didn't kill that white woman. But anyway, they're asking for character witnesses in his defense—what am I doing?" he says standing up. "You're deaf and dumb; and I'm even dumber for talking to you," he says as he walks off.

Mr. Nobody's eyes focus on the flyer.

As Bruno wanders aimlessly on the streets of New York, he is discovered by the Osmond family—a father and three sons. Bruno is such a fine specimen that the boys can't resist taking him in. They establish he is alone. The boys whistle to Bruno and he acknowledges by walking toward the van, wagging his tail. Mr. Osmond pulls off and the boys become saddened and beg him to stop. "Stop, Dad!"

"Dad please don't, he needs us," says one boy.

Another yells, "Look Dad, he's a stray, pull over!"

The third boy promises, "I won't ask for any toys for Christmas if we can have this dog."

Mr. Osmond raises an eyebrow and pulls over to the curb. "First condition, make sure he doesn't have a collar. Second condition, you boys solemnly swear to take good care of this dog."

"Yes!" the boys yell emphatically.

"We promise Dad."

"We got this Dad."

The boys slide the door open and rush towards Bruno, who greets them with licks on their faces. They walk Bruno back to the van and they all jump in.

"Now make sure he doesn't have a collar."

"No Dad, no collar," the first boy assures quickly as he conceals the collar and tag with his hands. They close the door and pull off. He removes the collar with the tag and conceals them under the seat.

Dave volunteers to approach Paul Goldberg to be Kwamina's defense attorney. Goldberg's office is on the second floor of a rundown, filthy tenement. Dave is cautious about where he steps and what he touches. At the top of the stairs, he notices the dirty glass framed door with the words "Paul Goldberg Attorney at Law." Dave peers in the door; the office is dimly lit. Dave knocks and receives no answer. "Goldberg?" he calls out.

In a faint voice, Goldberg answers, "Go away. I don't practice law anymore."

"Goldberg, just hear me out. We need to talk."

"Go away."

Dave, determined, opens the door and walks in to take in one of the most debasing sights he has seen in a long time. One of New York's finest criminal defense attorneys sits before him unkempt and reduced to alcoholism. Dave's first thought is to turn around and leave, but his instincts tell him that this is where he needs to be.

"Have a seat."

Dave looks around—clearly there is no seat.

"Want a drink?" Goldberg offers Dave a drink from his glass.

"No, no, no. I'm okay."

"You're wasting your time, but what's on your mind?" he asks while taking another drink.

"Can you not drink for a minute and hear me out?"

Goldberg looks at his watch and begins counting, "Fifty-nine, fifty-eight, fifty-seven…"

Dave interrupts, "Kwamina Washington."

Goldberg stops counting and says, "that kids gonna fry."

"I know this kid—he's innocent."

"Clearly you don't care about him if you're coming to me to defend him. Don't you know about me?"

"As a matter of fact I do. I know of you. To date, your record of wins as a defense attorney is unsurpassed."

"I haven't practiced in years."

"And your record still stands."

"Really? I'll drink to that."

"Yes. If anybody can pull this off Goldberg, it's you."

"You think so?"

"I know so."

"My last client committed suicide because I made a stupid mistake."

Dave leans over Goldberg's desk, looks him square in his eyes, and pounds the desk. "This kid is innocent!"

Goldberg becomes intimidated and leans back, then stands. He begins to pace back and forth with his hand on his chin. He spins around and points at Dave. "This is going to be a political case; I can see it. I can feel it in the atmosphere. The election is right around the corner. I know how they work in City Hall and I know more about the DA's office than they think I do. We're gonna have to work fast. I'll give you a list of things I'm going to need. We definitely don't want a jury trial because they can be bought. Leave your number."

"You gonna get your act together?"

"Don't you worry about my act."

The two men shake hands. "Thank you Mr. Goldberg. Thank you. Thank you so much."

"No, no, it's Paul. And I'll need a retainer of five grand."

"Not a problem."

Vivianna arrives at St. Ignatius Church. As she enters the big double doors, she blesses herself with holy water and genuflects. She hears the janitor singing Aaron Neville's version of "Ave Maria". Vivianna takes out her Rosary beads and kneels in front of the statue of the Blessed Virgin Mary. She signs herself with the cross and begins to pray, peering up at the statue. Tears begin to well up in her eyes and cascade down her face. "Holy Mary I can relate to your broken heart when you lost your son, Jesus; as I now may lose mine. Blessed Mary, mother of God, please go ask the Father to grant mercy. As a mother to you Blessed Mother, please guide me. Give me a sign."

At this moment, a woman enters the church bearing Christmas gifts. She trips and drops a box, distracting

Vivianna. Vivianna glances at the box and looks back at the statue with a puzzled expression. She thinks to herself, *the box, Bobby's box!*

Vivianna rushes through the apartment door and tosses her hat down. Hakeem and Sula are distracted momentarily by Vivianna, but resume their activities. Vivianna sits on the sofa in front of her enshrined gift, staring at it blankly. Hakeem notices something is about to go down. He looks at Sula, who then notices her mother's blank stare. They both stand and walk slowly towards their mother.

Hakeem asks uneasily, "Are you sure?"

Sula pleads, "Mama, no."

Vivianna replies, "Yes, it's time." Vivianna starts to rip the ribbon off the gift. Excitedly, the kids assist her with tearing the top off. They are captivated by the most exquisite Yvonne La Fleur hat they have ever seen.

In amazement, Hakeem exclaims, "Wow!"

Sula admires the hat and says, "Mama, it's beautiful."

In deep reflection, Vivianna smiles and says, "He always knew what pleases me." Vivianna reaches in the box, removes the hat, and holds it up with adoration. As she positions the hat to place it on her head, an envelope falls. Vivianna picks up the envelope and gingerly places the hat back in the box. She opens the envelope and to her surprise, she finds a stock certificate in Bobby's name that reflects a $10,000 investment at sixty-one shares. She drops her mouth in awe.

Hakeem asks curiously, "Mom, is that the receipt?"

"No, it's a stock certificate, and I think it's worth $10,000."

Jumping up and down Hakeem and Sula both scream, "We're rich, we're rich!"

"No, no. I'm not sure. I don't quite understand this, but if it is $10,000, we need to pay some bills. There is a name and number here."

Sula urges, "Call it, Mama; call it."

Vivianna dials the phone number listed on the stock certificate.

The receptionist answers, "Schuster & Young."

"Good day. May I speak to Christopher Reynolds please?"

"Sure ma'am. Hold please."

Christopher Reynolds answers, "Chris Reynolds."

"Mr. Reynolds, um, my name is Vivianna Washington. I have a stock certificate here with your signature and I don't know what to make of it."

"Okay ma'am. Let's back up. And the certificate is issued to whom?"

"Oh, uh, my husband, Bobby Washington."

"You've got to be kidding me! My very first client, Mr. Bobby. How is he?"

There is a pause from Vivianna.

"Mrs. Washington?"

"Mr. Reynolds, he is deceased."

Chris pauses.

"Hello, Mr. Reynolds?"

"Oh ma'am, I'm so sorry."

"I understand."

"He was an incredible gentleman."

"That he was."

"I'll never forget, it was my first day on the job. Mr. Bobby saw me and was adamant that I be his consultant. The firm was uneasy, as was I. Mr. Bobby handed me his investment, looked me square in the eyes, and said, 'Son, this is my life savings. I trust you will make it grow. I believe in you. Now don't contact me. I'll give you the address to the firehouse. Any and all correspondence should be sent there. I'll contact you when I feel the need.' And at that point Mrs. Washington, I believed in myself! Consequently, we set up a discretionary account, which gave me exclusive power to invest his money. It was then Mrs. Washington, I was pressured to perform! Now let's see what your stock is doing today. I'll need the certificate number, upper right hand corner, six digits."

"It's 492502."

Chris mumbles to himself while computing, "Okay let's see what we have. Closed at $88.75…$10,000 investment…61¢ split times seven. Mrs. Washington?"

Vivianna answers anxiously, "Yes, yes?"

"Are you sitting or standing?"

"Standing."

"You may want to have a seat."

Vivianna remains standing.

"That little piece of paper you have in your hand is worth $251,000.57." There is dead silence. "Mrs. Washington are you there?"

Vivianna falls back on the sofa. The kids look on in curious anticipation. Vivianna looks to her left at Sula, and then to her right at Hakeem. "We're not rich."

Hakeem sucks his teeth and sighs, "Ah man."

Sula says, "I knew it."

Vivianna screams, "We're filthy rich!" The three jubilantly embrace each other while jumping around in a circle. Chris hears the celebration and has a broad smile on his face.

In the day room of the jail, Kwamina sits at the head of a table speaking to six other inmates who give him their undivided attention. Kwamina's conversation is abruptly interrupted by a detestable guard. "Hey, dead man talking!" Everyone stops their conversations and divert their attention to the guard. "Yeah you cracklin," pointing at Kwamina. "Fry boy…"

Some hateful inmates are laughing in the background while Kwamina's friends are embarrassed. One of the inmates says, "Damn dog, that's messed up."

Kwamina ashamed and embarrassed, puts his head down. Fueled by the attention he is receiving from the racist inmates, the guard continues his onslaught of insults.

While sniffing the air he jeers, "Hmmm cracklin, smells like burning skin. Can't wait to cook another coon. The state of New York is gonna serve cooked coon soon. Wait…wait…I can't hold your Christmas gift much longer, batteries included. It's burning me up! I don't think you'll be here that long so check this out." The guard then demonstrates a doll being electrocuted in a toy electric chair. Kwamina pounds the table in anger.

Later that night Kwamina is troubled in his sleep and is awakened by a nightmare. In his dream, Kwamina is seated and strapped in the electric chair while his family helplessly observes through a glass partition. Vivianna is standing with both palms pressed against the glass while screaming the words "NO, NO, NO!" The detestable guard throws the switch while laughing uncontrollably. Kwamina wakes in a cold sweat. Shaken by the nightmare, he tries to compose himself by standing up. While breathing heavily and in deep thought, he hears his father's voice saying, "Son, no weapon formed against you shall prosper. Remember Psalms 23:4."

Kwamina speaks aloud, "What was I thinking? Dad, I can survive with the lessons you taught me; sometimes I just get weak," falling to his knees in prayer. "Father God Jehovah, as I strive to be righteous my Father, my life has been touched by some unfortunate events; but when I reflect Father, more fulfilling events by far. Is my work done here? Who am I to question you? Thy kingdom come, thy will be done, on Earth as it is in Heaven. Life is good thanks to you Heavenly Father, no matter it's time. I pray you continue to bless and keep my family strong. Amen."

Mr. Hessler sits at the kitchen table reading the morning paper. Mrs. Hessler sits across from him sipping her coffee. Mrs. Hessler asks, "Ron, that young boy's name is Kwamina. Don't you miss him? My instincts tell me he didn't do it. Baby, would you do me a favor?"

Mr. Hessler folds one end of the paper down to look at his wife.

"Would you find out what you could that may help his case? You're the best. If you do that for me, I'll prepare your favorite peach cobbler. It'll knock your socks off!"

"With the edges slightly burnt?"

"You got it!"

Hessler is on the steps of the DA's office when he is greeted by some of his former colleagues.

A patrolman asks, "Hey Detective Hessler, how's retirement?"

"Boring," Hessler replies.

"Tired of being a house husband already?"

A detective wants to know, "Hey Ron, can we ever get rid of you?"

"Not as long as you're here screwing things up."

Entering the building, Hessler walks over to the desk sergeant. With hands extended, the desk sergeant asks, "Hey Ron, what brings you out of retirement?"

"I need to look at the Kwamina Washington file. Who's got that case?"

"Lamarque's got that case, but he's been out."

"Good, but I still need to see that file."

The desk sergeant hands Hessler the key, looks around, and pats him on the shoulder saying, "If anyone can seal that nigger's fate, it's you."

"Yeah, yeah."

Locating a quiet, inconspicuous corner, Hessler flips through the file while taking notes. "Hmmm, interesting."

When Mr. Hessler returns home, he notices his wife is busy in the kitchen preparing his favorite peach cobbler. Realizing he's calling someone, she begins to ease drop.

Goldberg answers his telephone, "Goldberg."

Hessler replies, "I have some information that may help your Washington case. And for what it's worth, I don't think it went down like that."

"Who is this?"

"I can't testify because of my position with the force. I'd like to remain anonymous."

"I'll respect that. What do you have?"

Hessler, realizing his wife is quiet, leans back, then resumes his conversation. "For starters, evidence was omitted. There was a dog at the scene that attacked Officer Wilson, who was treated later that day for a dog bite. Your client, on the other hand was treated for a gsw, not a dog bite. You figure that out; could be an angle."

"Okay," Goldberg says as he writes frantically.

"This dog in question was Mrs. Marullo's German Shepherd. I found out he answers to the name Bruno. He has somehow disappeared.

"Why would they not mention the dog?"

"To spare embarrassment and to avoid losing sick days."

"Embarrassment, I don't understand."

"Putting this scene together in my head, I would say the dog was attacking Wilson while Firmin was on the ground tussling with your client. It could have been Firmin who was shot, but your client was in the wrong position when the gun was fired. As a result he caught a bullet in the ass. Furthermore, mugging, I think not. All of Mrs. Marullo's valuables were intact: mink, diamond earrings, necklace, and ring, Cartier watch, and $761 in her purse. I know these thugs; they can strip you to your drawers in seconds."

"This is good. This is real good. I'm gonna need everything I can get to help this kid. Thank you."

"If I can find anything else I'll pass it on."

Mrs. Hessler enters the room wiping her hands. From behind, she embraces her husband. "You did the right thing. Don't you feel better now?"

"Yeah I guess so. I'll feel a whole lot better with some peach cobbler and a cup of coffee."

Mr. Osmond is in his den seated in front of the television watching the morning news. Phil reports,

"The Kwamina Washington case took a bizarre twist today when Defense Attorney Paul Goldberg contacted us to assist in locating Mrs. Loretta Marullo's dog, Bruno," while showing Bruno's picture, "who was believed to have been at the scene of Mrs. Marullo's murder. Connie Anderson has this report."

"Thank you Phil. We are here with Attorney Goldberg and my question is, Counselor, is it plausible that a canine be a witness in a murder case?"

"Well yes Connie. I'm pulling out all the stops. I'll do whatever it takes to prove my clients' innocence."

"But Counselor, a dog can't talk."

"Good point but I have an angle here. I've been in touch with a dog expert who will testify; but I do need this dog."

"Okay, and I understand you are offering a reward."

"Yes $5,000."

"Anyone with information on the whereabouts of Bruno, you can be $5,000 richer by contacting Attorney Goldberg at 555-5127. Phil…"

"Connie what's the prosecuting attorney's take on this?"

"As a matter of fact, we did contact Attorney Charles Fisks' office. He refused to comment on camera, but he did offer this: 'Connie this is an open and shut case. Goldberg is desperate and is barking up the wrong tree, excuse the pun.'"

While chuckling, Phil says, "I just hope Attorney Goldberg knows what he's doing or his case will be going to the dogs. He's got his work cut out for him."

Monica, the other anchor, adds, "Well, he's got a remarkable record of wins. I just don't know."

"And other breaking news—"

In awe, Mr. Osmond turns off the television and looks at Bruno. "Bruno?" At the sound of his name, Bruno lifts his head with ears erect and looks directly at Mr. Osmond. "Those boys," he groans as he shakes his head and clenches his teeth.

Mr. Osmond proceeds to dial Goldberg's phone number. Goldberg has answered crank calls all day and is growing quite annoyed. "Is it a German Shepherd?"

"Yes Mr. Goldberg, it is. I have your dog."

"Yeah, you and about three hundred other quacks outside with every breed of dog imaginable. I'm only seeing German Shepherds. Please don't waste my time. I'm at 7634 Kingsport Street."

Mr. Osmond pulls up to the obvious address and notices a line of people with dogs wrapped around the corner. Everyone is trying to convince their dog that his name is Bruno. One person is even trying hypnosis. Before he can park, Mr. Osmond hears Goldberg make an announcement to the crowd. "I am only seeing German Shepherds. All you other people please go home."

One person says, "Mr. Goldberg you've got to see this. This is going to clench it for ya."

"Okay, what?" Goldberg reluctantly acquiesces.

"Okay, watch this, watch this." With a quick snap of his fingers, he immediately calls Bruno's name, giving the illusion that the dog is responding to the name Bruno. "Bruno." He then looks at Goldberg and says excitedly, "It gets better." The owner points his finger straight up while looking at his dog. "Now Bruno, is Kwamina Washington innocent?"

The dog barks.

"A simple yes would have been fine. He said 'hell yes.'"

Goldberg grabs the man by his shirt and pushes him away. "Get out of here."

"I'll take $500."

"Get out of here you bum!"

The crowd disperses. Only two Shepherds remain in line. Bruno and Mr. Osmond are still in the van. Mr. Osmond exits the van and catches Goldberg's attention. "Mr. Goldberg, I have your dog."

"Well we're down to three. We'll see what we've got. You're dog #1, you're dog #2," looking at Mr. Osmond, "and dog #3 you can remain in your van. I'm going to the top of these stairs and I'll call for your dog. If he acknowledges, please come up the stairs; you're a contender. If not, please leave." Goldberg goes to the top of the stairs and turns around. Looking at dog #1 he calls out, "Bruno." Dog #1 doesn't respond. The real Bruno hears his name and tries to escape from the van. He begins to pace and whimper.

The first Shepherd owner has his back to Goldberg and is pleading with his dog, "I need this money. Please go up the stairs. Attack, sick him boy."

Goldberg demands, "Get out of here."

The first Shepherd owner leashes his dog and leaves. As the second Shepherd owner gets into position, Mr. Osmond slides the van door open.

While looking at dog #2, Goldberg calls out again, "Bruno." The real Bruno lunges out of the van and runs up the stairs to Goldberg. "By golly I think we have Bruno," scratching Bruno's head and petting him.

Mr. Osmond follows Bruno up the stairs.

"I will notify Bruno's family for positive ID. Once confirmed, I will contact you to claim your reward."

"Oh no. I don't want your reward. Let's leave it at that; he's yours. I don't want any trouble."

CHAPTER 7

Kwamina's Trial

Ms. Ola and Mr. Jessie enter the courtroom. Mr. Jessie uses his cane while he leads Ms. Ola with his free arm. Ms. Ola orders, "Jessie, bring me to the front so I could see everything."

Mr. Jessie replies, "If you sat in the judge's lap you couldn't see him!"

"Shut up you ole decrepit gimp leg dog. Now get me to a good seat."

Mr. Jessie steps back and allows Ms. Ola to enter a row of seats. Not seeing the young woman, Ms. Ola accidentally sits in her lap. "Oh, excuse me sir."

"Does that look like a man to you? That's a pretty young lady. Ain't nothing manish about that. Yes indeed!"

There is a knock on the courtroom doors, which is strange. The bailiff pushes the doors open and in comes Smukie. With a British accent he says, "Top of the morning to you sir. Straighten that tie," as he straightens the bailiff's tie. Smukie makes his way to the front of the courtroom, looking for Kwamina. The two happen to make eye contact and exchange smiles. At that instance, Smukie recognizes the judge as one of this latest victims. The judge looks up just in time to see Smukie uneasily backing out.

While shaking his finger, the judge asks, "Don't I know you?"

"No sir. I don't believe you do," he answers while turning around and running out of the courtroom.

The bailiff calls out, "Your honor, case #96-42777, State of New York verses Kwamina Washington."

Judge Jemison says, "For the record gentlemen, identify yourselves; you know the procedures. Oh, Mr. Goldberg, good to see you back."

"Thank you your honor."

With a tinge of jealousy, Charles Fisk announces, "For the state, Charles Fisk, chief prosecutor."

"And for the defense your honor, just Paul Goldberg," Goldberg says, downplaying Fisk's sarcasm.

"I've read the charges gentlemen. Please proceed Mr. Fisk, with your opening statement."

"Thank you your honor. The state is here to prove that on October 29, 1993, at approximately 10:30 am, a prominent citizen, I would even go as far as saying an icon in her community, Mrs. Loretta Marullo, was viciously mugged and murdered by the defendant, Kwamina Washington." All the while, Fisk is pacing back and forth with a cocky arrogance.

Goldberg interjects, "I object."

"Sustained."

Fisk continues, "As evidence, the state has the eye witness testimonies of two New York police officers." Fisk points at the officers and they nod in agreement. "Officer Gary Wilson, a five-year veteran, and Officer Peter Firmin, a fifteen-year veteran. To further strengthen our case is the death certificate from the New York City Coroner's Office, which states that Mrs. Marullo's death was a homicide," he says as he reads the death certificate and looks at Goldberg. "The facts will reveal that on said morning, Mrs. Marullo was ambushed by the defendant in broad daylight. The two police officers witnessed this, and immediately came to her rescue, foiling the defendant's calculated attack. A fight ensued and the defendant was wounded while resisting arrest. He fled the scene and was later apprehended and charged with first degree murder and felony fleeing." Fisk returns to his seat.

"Thank you Mr. Fisk. Looking at Goldberg, Judge Jemison says, "The stage is yours. Have at it."

Goldberg stands and addresses the judge directly. "Thank you. Your honor, the defense is here to prove that my client, Kwamina Washington, is innocent of all charges. We will establish his innocence first by refuting the questionable testimonies of the eye witnesses due to the considerable distance involved. Furthermore, our evidence will reveal no mugging occurred simply because Mrs. Marullo's valuables were completely intact. As far as the fight mentioned, my client was acting out of self-defense. Confused and wounded, my client fled the scene and later turned himself in. My client's deposition will state that he was attempting to save Mrs. Marullo's life, not take it."

Fisk chuckles aloud while the court mumbles.

"Order."

"In conclusion, the defense has expert testimony to refute the coroner's report."

"Thank you Mr. Goldberg. Let's get this show on the road. Fisk, call your first witness."

"Your honor the state calls eye witness Officer Gary Wilson to the stand."

The bailiff swears the officer in. "Officer Wilson to the stand. Raise your right hand please. Do you swear the testimony you are about to give is the truth, the whole truth, and nothing but the truth so help you God?"

With hand raised, Officer Wilson says, "I do."

"Take the stand and state your name," orders the bailiff.

"Gary Wilson."

Officer Wilson takes the stand.

Judge Jemison says, "Proceed."

Fisk asks, "Officer Wilson can you point out the person you witnessed murder Mrs. Marullo?"

"Your honor, I object."

"Fisk, rephrase that question; and you know better."

"Officer Wilson do you recognize the alleged suspect you witnessed murder Mrs. Marullo?"

"Your honor, I object. The cause of Mrs. Marullo's death is being challenged."

"Sustained," the judge says, as he points at Fisk. "One more time and I'll hold you in contempt. I'm not in the playing mood. And why the theatrics? This is not a jury trial."

"Okay Officer Wilson, can you identify the suspect?"

"Yes, he's right there," he says while pointing at Kwamina.

"And on that day how close were you to the suspect? How could you make a positive ID?"

"Close enough to smell his bad breath."

Mixed reactions come from the court.

"For the record, what did you see that morning?"

"Well, my partner and I were on patrol."

"Which partner are you speaking of?"

"Peter, right there."

"Let the records show, my witness is identifying Officer Peter Firmin. Okay proceed."

"We were at a light on the corner of Park and 52nd when we saw this black kid on the ground punching an elderly white woman in the chest."

Goldberg interrupts, "Objection your honor, race is irrelevant."

"Overruled. Allow the witness to establish the physical characteristics of the suspect. Proceed Mr. Fisk."

"Thank you your honor. Officer Wilson you may continue."

"Like I was saying, we were clearing pedestrians on our right to make a right turn, and I almost choked on my jelly donut," everyone laughs and the judge shakes his head, "when in broad daylight, we see him beating this old woman to death."

"Objection your honor, conjecture."

"Sustained; strike. The judge becomes disgusted with Wilson and orders, "Structure your questions so he can answer yes or no."

"Actually, I have no further questions for this witness."

"Mr. Goldberg would you like to cross?"

"No your honor, I'll pass."

Fisk asks slyly, "Knowing you're done?"

"Um no, knowing his IQ."

"Officer Wilson you're dismissed. Mr. Fisk call your next witness."

"The state calls fifteen-year veteran, Officer Peter Firmin."

The bailiff swears Officer Firmin in. "Raise your right hand. Do you swear the testimony you are about to give is the truth, the whole truth, and nothing but the truth so help you God?"

Officer Firmin raises his right hand and says, "I do."

"Take the stand and state your name."

"Peter Firmin."

Judge Jemison says, "Proceed."

Fisk asks, "Officer Firmin would you describe to the court what you eye witnessed on the morning in question?"

"Sure. The morning of October 29, 1993, at approximately 10:30 a.m., my partner Wilson and I were on routine patrol where I was the passenger in unit 203. As he stated earlier, we were on Park and 52nd, making a right turn onto Park when I observed the defendant."

Fisk interrupts by asking, "Officer Firmin is that person in this courtroom? Can you identify him?"

"Yes, that's him right there," he says while pointing at Kwamina.

"For the record, my witness is identifying Kwamina Washington, the defendant." Fisk turns back to Firmin, "How can you be sure?"

"Because I wrestled him to the ground moments later."

"Continue."

"What we witnessed, was the defendant pushing the victim to the ground, whom we later found out to be Mrs. Marullo. We then code one to the scene so as not to alarm the defendant, with hopes of apprehending him. We observed the perpetrator—"

Goldberg interrupts, "Objection your honor. My client is a suspect."

"Sustained. Officer Firmin, refer to Mr. Washington as the defendant or suspect."

"We observed the suspect desperately searching through the victim's coat and purse. He then proceeded to choke her and punch her in the chest. Upon arriving at the scene, I immediately attempted to subdue the suspect. He resisted and was going for my gun when he was subsequently wounded by Wilson. I lost my grip and the suspect fled the scene. Our attention was then diverted to the victim and I proceeded to call in the incident."

"Now Officer Firmin, what were your observations of the victim?"

"She was clearly unconscious. She may have even been dead. There was nothing we could do but secure the area and wait for the emergency unit."

"Thank you for that credible testimony Officer Firmin."

"Mr. Goldberg?" the judge asks.

"Oh yeah, I want this one. Officer Firmin are you certain you saw my client pushing Mrs. Marullo to the ground, or could he have been trying to break her fall, and simply fell on top of her?"

"Nice try Goldberg. I know what I saw; he pushed her down."

"Officer Firmin, you were approximately three hundred feet away and you observed all of this?"

"Yeah."

"And you also observed my client going through Mrs. Marullo's belongings?"

"Yes."

"Again three hundred feet away?"

"At this point two ninety eight."

"Well that's odd because nothing was missing. Do you think he was simply rearranging her contents for her?"

The court laughs and Officer Firmin squirms in his seat.

"Officer Firmin, approximately how far away were you when you observed my client choking Mrs. Marullo?"

"Only about twenty feet."

"Did my client have one or two hands around Mrs. Marullo's neck?"

"One hand."

"Okay, choking her with one hand while the other hand was busy doing what, tickling her?"

The court laughs again.

Fisk becomes annoyed and says, "Your honor I object. He is leading my witness, trying to make a mockery of his testimony."

"Sustained, and I'd advise your witness not to follow his lead and give yes or no answers."

Goldberg says, "Now calm down Counselor. You'll have plenty of time to get upset."

Firmin loses his control and blurts out, "I was ten feet away when I saw him punch her in the chest. You didn't ask me about that did you?"

"Now Officer Firmin, did it ever strike you as being odd that when you pulled up in a squad car, in full uniform, with baton drawn, that my client didn't get up and run? Did it ever dawn on you that something was strange about this?"

Firmin refuses to answer and looks at Fisk.

"Officer Firmin, we're waiting."

The judge says, "Officer Firmin answer the question."

"Nah," Firmin mumbles.

"Sir, we can't hear you."

"I said no!"

"Did you order my client to cease and desist?"

"No because—"

Fisk interrupts and points at Firmin, "Yes or no answers."

"No."

"So Officer Firmin, you immediately assumed this was a mugging in progress and you attacked my client?"

"Objection your honor. Officer Firmin was merely doing his job in trying to protect Mrs. Marullo."

"Sustained. Mr. Goldberg," the judge says in a stern voice while giving him a warning look.

"Yes, your honor. Officer Firmin, were you attempting to cuff my client, or did you in fact have him in a choke hold?"

While looking at Firmin, Fisk says, "Yes or no."

"No, I wasn't trying to cuff him and yes, I had him in a choke hold."

"Okay Officer Firmin, you're alluding to the fact that this young man, half your size was able to get out of your choke hold?"

Standing, "Yeah because the little bastard was going for my gun. That's why Wilson shot him in the ass."

"Order! I will not allow this. Officer Firmin, one more outburst like that and you'll be dismissed."

Fisk looks at his witness and positions his palms down as if telling him to calm down.

"Okay now Officer Firmin, to sum things up to the best of your recollection, the sequence of events are as follows: my client pushed Mrs. Marullo to the ground, went through her belongings, choked her, punched her in the chest, was shot, then fled. Am I accurate in this sequence?"

"Yeah, I would say that's accurate."

"That'll be all for now Officer Firmin."

"Okay Mr. Goldberg, the ball's in your court."

"At this time your honor the defense would like to establish the character of my client with a series of character witnesses, and end with expert testimonies in his defense. Your honor, the defense calls Vinh Nguyen to the stand."

Goldberg notices Mr. Nguyen sitting in the front and motions him to the witness stand. As Mr. Nguyen walks toward to the stand he addresses the judge. "Your honor, Kwanama goot, goot nigga. He goot nigga like you."

Judge Jemison is clearly aghast. Fisk is grinning from ear to ear with his eyes wide open. Goldberg is in shock, and comes to Mr. Nguyen's aid.

"Mr. Nguyen," Goldberg says, while putting his finger to his lips, "your honor, I know it doesn't sound good, but in the Vietnamese dialect, that word means good person and is pronounced *gooniga*. Mr. Nguyen, thank you for your testimony. Please be seated."

As Mr. Nguyen returns to his seat, he looks at Kwamina, nodding his head and smiling.

"The defense calls the next character witness, Jessie Hawkins."

Mr. Jessie slowly and feebly stands, trembling while balancing his weight on his cane.

"To the stand Mr. Hawkins."

"Your honor to the stand? I'm lucky I can stand. And I know I can't climb those stairs, but I can tell you from here," he says as he points his cane toward Kwamina. "That's a good boy and it's not in his nature to do something like this your honor."

"Thank you for your testimony Mr. Hawkins. Speaking of nature, nature calls. Excuse me while I take a quick nature break. Mr. Goldberg call your next witness."

"Defense calls its next character witness Ms. Ola Jenkins to the stand please."

"Praise the Lord," Ms. Ola says as she stands. Ms. Ola straightens her dress, adjusts her wig, and grabs her purse. She then slides to the center aisle and acknowledges a man whom she presumes to be the young woman she sat on. "And excuse me ma'am," she says proudly as she walks toward the judge's seat.

Goldberg is preoccupied with his files and doesn't notice Ms. Ola sitting in the judge's chair.

"My word! This is a nice chair," she says as she rocks back and forth. Looking around she asks, "Where da judge at?"

Goldberg looks up when he hears Ms. Ola's question. "No Ms. Jenkins, over there."

The bailiff immediately assists Ms. Ola to the right chair as the judge returns.

"Where the judge?"

"Right there ma'am," the bailiff answers.

Looking at the judge and pointing to Goldberg, Ms. Ola says, "Your honor, y'all gotta get this boy outta jail. He ain't gettin no sun. Look how pale he is poor baby."

The judge is confused and Goldberg immediately interrupts. "Ms. Jenkins, no. I'm Mr. Paul Goldberg, Kwamina's attorney. Kwamina is seated right here."

The judge is humored.

"Now Ms. Jenkins, would you please share with the court today your testimony on Kwamina Washington's behalf?"

Looking in Fisks direction, she begins her testimony, "Mr. Goldbird." Goldberg sidesteps in her line of vision before the judge notices. "I may not see too good, but what I hear with these ears," touching her ears, "and feel in this heart," patting her chest, "is far better than 20/20 hearing or vision. What my heart feels is a God fearing, praise the Lord, good boy. And all I hear about him is good. They got a bunch of 'em in my neighborhood that wouldn't make good firewood for hell! She turns back to the judge and points to the bailiff. "That boy is righteous and to know him is to love him bless his heart! Your honor, you know the kind of boy I'm talkin' about."

The judge nods, "Yes."

"Thank you Ms. Jenkins for that testimony. You're dismissed. Bailiff…" The defense calls the next witness, Mr. Stan, 'the stutter,'" sounding unsure, "Pane."

Almost everyone who knows Stan has a comment or makes a gesture.

"Are they serious?"

"We'll be in here 'til lunch."

"Oh no…"

"Oh my God," while stuttering and mocking Stan.

"Who put him up to this?"

"Who spoke for him to do this?"

Goldberg says, "Can't be that bad," as he turns around. Goldberg addresses Stan, "For the record, please state your name."

Stand begins to stutter uncontrollably, "S…"

Goldberg assists him, "Stan." Goldberg and Kwamina look at each other and speak simultaneously. "It's gonna be bad!"

Kwamina instructs him, "Take a deep breath and relax. It's gonna be alright."

"We are going to forget 'the stutter.' Last name please."

"P…" he stutters again.

"Pane," Goldberg says.

Stan nods an exaggerated yes!

"Now what can you tell me about my client in sixty seconds?" Goldberg asks while looking at his watch.

The court laughs.

"He…is…g…"

The court reporter continuously pecks at one key until Stan finishes a word.

Goldberg assists, "Good! He is good. Okay, thank you Mr. Pane. You're dismissed."

The court reporter drops a pencil and leans over to retrieve it; exposing her thigh.

"Damn!" Stan says very clearly.

Goldberg looks at Stan in total surprise; Kwamina chuckles.

"Your honor, the defense calls character witness Tony Collatta to the stand."

No one responds, so the bailiff summons Mr. Collatta. "Mr. Tony Collatta. Is there a Tony Collatta?"

Tony jumps up in the back of the courtroom. "Yo, yo. That could be me. You wanna spell Collatta?"

While looking at his pad the bailiff spells, "C-O-L-L-A-T-T-A."

"Hey, none other than the one and only, the original, AKA Mr. Penis Collatta. And by the way, the two L's are for luv the ladies," he says as he nods his head from side to side.

The bailiff gestures for Tony to proceed to the stand. Tony walks into the middle of the aisle primping; straightens his shirt, combs his hair, smoothes over his eyebrows with his wet fingers, and puts his sunglasses on. He then proceeds to walk to the stand with a gangster strut.

Judge Jemison orders, "Loose the shades."

Tony spins on one heel and addresses the judge. "Yo, yo that's cool your hipness. This is yo world. I'm just a squirrel trying to get my next nut," he says as he makes a pelvic thrust gesture.

"Have a seat."

Tony sits down, pulls out a pack of cigarettes, and begins to pop them. The judge gives him a look and he immediately puts the cigarettes back in his pocket. Tony then crosses his legs and waits for Goldberg to approach him.

"Mr. Collatta, you are here as a character witness for Kwamina Washington. Please tell us in your own words what you know about Mr. Washington's character."

"Now let me get this right. You did say in my own words?"

"Um, yeah," Goldberg says with uncertainty.

"Cool. Okay, yo check this out. My man Kwam is da coolest yo. I mean, he's fly. He come on like good dope. I seen him thread better than that though. Now look at him, my man phat!"

The judge and attorneys are totally confused. The court reporter sits with her mouth wide open in expressionless awe.

"Mr. Collatta, the court thanks you for that, I think. You may step down."

Tony stands, steps down, and walks toward Kwamina. "Gimme dat double dap dog!" With clenched fists Tony and Kwamina dap each other up and down. Tony slips Kwamina the key to his cuffs. "Smukie sends his love." Tony winks at Kwamina then swiftly exits the courtroom in his gangster strut.

"What's this?" Kwamina whispers to himself while holding the keys.

The bailiff sees the keys and reaches into his pocket, realizing they are the keys to Kwamina's handcuffs. The bailiff looks for Tony who just exited through the back door. The bailiff walks over to Kwamina and snatches the keys from him.

"Your honor, the defense calls its last character witness, Paula McMurray to the stand."

Paula walks to the stand as she is being noticed by Fisk. Fisk does a double take, and everyone realizes Paula has Down's syndrome. He throws his file on the table in front of him and extends his arms in exasperation, showing his frustration.

"Ms. Mcurray, um, unfortunately, we cannot use you as a character witness because, uh," he pauses, not wanting to insult her; he starts fumbling through his papers.

Paula finishes his sentence, "because I'm retarded."

Goldberg looks down sadly.

"I know I can't be a witness, but I am a witness for my friend. I know he is good. He is good to me every time I see him. I know that he," pointing to Fisk, "is bad." "And he," pointing to Kwamina, "could not hurt anyone because of his heart," she continues as she places her hand over her heart. Paula then stands and looks directly at Kwamina with tears in her eyes. Kwamina gazes back at her with tears welling in his eyes. Kwamina wipes his eyes with his cuffed hands.

Paula says, "Kwamina, I love you."

Kwamina extends his cuffed hands with open palms and mouths the words, "I love you, too."

"And your honor if you can't feel the love of my friend, then you're retarded."

The judge rears back in astonishment; Goldberg cringes. "Ms. McMurray, thank you for your testimony," Goldberg says quickly as he gestures for Paula to leave the stand.

"Your honor, prosecution graciously agreed to allow this letter from Jeremiah Duplesis to be used on behalf of my client's character."

The judge is impressed and sighs, "Jeremiah Duplesis, Giants quarterback—oh wow!"

Goldberg reads, "Dear Honorable Judge Martin Jemison: My misfortune is that my busy athletic schedule would not permit my presence to give testimony on behalf of my dear brother Kwamina Washington. However, my fortune commenced when I was adopted into the Washington family. The malicious crime that Kwamina is being charged with is not conducive of the loving, God fearing, nurturing environment he was raised in. This is a gross misrepresentation of my brother's character. I will be willing to bet my Super Bowl ring that Kwamina didn't commit this crime. I beseech you to utilize every resource at your disposal in adjudicating these proceedings. Thank you."

When Goldberg finishes the letter, he notices the judge staring into space. "Very impressive. Thank you for sharing that with us."

"Your honor that'll wrap up character witnesses. Defense would like to proceed with expert testimonies. The defense calls Dr. Richard Stevenson to the stand."

The bailiff calls, "Dr. Richard Stevenson."

No one answers.

Fisk injects, "Oh, I guess the rec room at Bellevue is empty now."

The judge addresses the bailiff, "Just check the hallway."

The bailiff goes into the hallway. He opens one door as someone opens the other door. At that moment, a handsome, statuesque, well-dressed gentleman emerges through the double doors. As he proceeds toward the witness stand, he is noticed by everyone; heads turn and women gawk. He notices the Washington family in the front row. Dr. Stevenson stops, and acknowledges Vivianna. He nods at Vivianna and gives her a reassuring touch on the shoulder. She touches his hand.

Vivianna mouths the words, "Thank you."

He then nods at Hakeem, who shrugs his shoulders. He makes eye contact with Sula and she smiles.

Dr. Stevenson blows her a kiss and she is totally confused. He winks at her and she instantly realizes who he is!

Vivianna leans forward and whispers, "Who is that?"

Sula says excitedly, "Mama, that's Mr. Nobody!"

Hakeem dismisses Sula and says, "Girl, you're crazy. Mr. Nobody is a bum."

When Dr. Stevenson passes the defense table, he acknowledges Kwamina with a thumbs up. Kwamina nods a "thank you." Kwamina turns around and looks at his mom.

Kwamina mouths, "Who's that?"

"Mr. Nobody," Vivianna replies visibly but not audibly.

Goldberg says, "For the record sir, your name."

"Your honor, I am Dr. Richard M. Stevenson."

Judge Jemison asks excitedly, "The Dr. Richard Stevenson?"

"Yes your honor."

"No, I am honored!"

Fisk gives the judge a look of disgust.

"And Dr. Stevenson, what qualifies you to give testimony on behalf of Kwamina Washington?"

"My qualifications are as follows: MD, PhD, with a six-year tenure teaching forensic pathology at Columbia University, a two year stint at Meharry teaching gross anatomy, and a one-time nomination for the Nobel Peace Prize for my research and writings on DNA. I am the quintessential lecturer in my field, and I am on the International Board of Editors for The American Journal of Forensic Medicine and Pathology."

Standing with excitement, Judge Jemison adds, "And don't forget your articles in The New England Journal of Medicine—helped me with a very difficult case. I'd like to speak with you after these proceedings."

Fisk is clearly agitated with the bias the judge is showing and slams his file on his desk.

Goldberg says matter of factly, "I would say you're pretty well qualified to testify in this case."

"Your honor, I challenge his qualifications."

The judge looks at Goldberg, Goldberg looks at Fisk.

"Go right ahead," Goldberg offers with a welcoming hand.

"Dr. Stevenson, medical board number?"

"Ny1977."

"You did teach at the universities, and you are a medical doctor. But, no one we interviewed has seen or heard from you in the last three years; you just disappeared. Drugs maybe, or perhaps alcohol? Will you explain to the court your three-year hiatus?" Fisk walks away, closes his file, and throws a sly, cocky grin at Goldberg.

The judge looks at Dr. Stevenson as he places his face in his hands. At this moment, Goldberg is concerned. The courtroom is so quiet with anticipation that you could hear a pin drop. Dr. Stevenson takes a moment. The judge insists, "Dr. Stevenson, take your time."

Dr. Stevenson removes his hands and exposes the tears in his eyes. He looks down, muttering and visibly shaken, "It's a painful memory, but, I owe it to the court. It was September 7, 1990. I was in class and my

TA interrupted me to take an emergency phone call. My first thought was my family—my wife and three children. On the other end of the phone was State Trooper Jerry Mullins who informed me of an accident involving my family. Trooper Mullins instructed me to meet him at NYU Downtown and refused to give me any more details. Upon arriving at the emergency room area, I asked for Trooper Mullins who wasn't there; so I identified myself and asked for the Stevenson family. For some reason, the staff repudiated my request to see my family. Noticing my desperate plea, a janitor mopping the floor offered his assistance; he motioned me to follow him.

Walking down a long corridor, which seemed endless, my eyes then focused above two double doors, the word Morgue. I felt like my life as I had known it was being sucked out of me. At that point, I knew I lost my soul and my will to live. I immediately started trembling in horror. I couldn't find the strength to walk through those doors. I was wishing this was a dream and I would wake up. I had to face this reality and walk into my worst nightmare! I then proceeded through the doors to see four gurneys varying in sizes covered with sheets. These gurneys held my wife and three children. At this point, I asked God to awaken me from my nightmare, but he didn't. I walked over to the longest gurney, pulled the sheet back, and fell to my knees. My mind instantly went to sleep in the condition called a catatonic stupor. I was awakened three years later by the love of that little girl right there," he says as he points to Sula, "who reminded me so much of my little Joi, who would be her age about now. The power of love brought me back. The respect

I have for these kids is insurmountable. Realizing the eldest needed my help, I recovered. I am back, and I am ready!" he says with defiance as he looks at Fisk.

The judge catches himself overcome with excitement and regains his composure. Fisk has a blank look on his face and seats himself. The court cheers.

Goldberg asks, "Dr. Stevenson, would you share with the court how you applied your expertise," looking at Fisk, "to this case?"

Dr. Stevenson puts on his reading glasses and opens a folder. When he puts his glasses on, a woman in the courtroom makes a flirtatious sound of approval.

"Your honor," looking at the judge, "Mr. Goldberg," looking at Goldberg, "after reviewing the information presented in the autopsy report, I have concluded: first, there was no evidence of trauma or bruising of the infra hyoid, longus capitus, or longus colli muscles in the neck to support strangulation."

"Now Dr. Stevenson, would you say Mrs. Marullo was beaten to death?"

"No, and to refute the allegations made by the officers that Mrs. Marullo was punched in the chest, I found no contusions to support trauma to the chest area. However, the pericardial thump, which can convert a fibrillation to a normal heart beat, could have easily confused the officers."

"Dr. Stevenson, will you explain Mrs. Marullo's fractured rib?"

"Now, the fractured rib probably was a result of compressions administered by CPR."

"Are there any additional findings you'd care to share with the court?"

"Yes, finally, the key is the high value of adrenaline in Mrs. Marullo's blood; undetected by the coroner. Excess amounts of adrenaline can shock the heart into the condition I mentioned earlier, ventricular fibrillation. Some of the effects of adrenaline are increase in the rate and strength of the heartbeat, and vasoconstriction, which would stress a diseased heart. In conclusion, the woman was simply, scared to death."

"Very interesting Dr. Stevenson. Now, if you were the coroner in this case, how would you have classified Mrs. Marullo's death?"

"Mrs. Marullo's medical records indicated that she had a history of coronary artery disease. Her medications indicate the magnitude of her disease, that is her use of nitroglycerin. I believe in her dying breath, she was telling Kwamina to locate her nitro. Hence, explaining him going through her purse. In lieu of the circumstances and testimonies given, I would say induced accidental death."

"Dr. Stevenson, thank you for that riveting testimony."

"Wait, wait, wait—one more statement. If anyone should be on trial, it should be the two officers. In my professional opinion, had Kwamina been allowed to continue administering CPR on Mrs. Marullo, her chances of survival would have been much greater."

"Thanks again, Dr. Stevenson."

"Mr. Fisk, do you care to cross?"

"Why bother, obviously you're sold," Fisk says with attitude.

"Mr. Fisk I'm going to strike, and you're lucky I don't hold you in contempt. Dr. Stevenson you're dismissed."

The assistant DA brings to Fisk's attention a document in a folder. Fisk abruptly grabs the folder and shuts it. "I'll get rid of this."

While looking at Fisk with disgust, the assistant DA says, "I quit. I'm not going to be a part of this lynching."

Jemison barely overhears the comment. "What did you say?"

"Uh, nothing your honor. And for the record, I'm dismissing myself from this case," he says as he closes his briefcase and exits the courtroom.

The judge gives Fisk a quizzical look as Fisk shoves the folder in his briefcase and closes it. Reporters rush the assistant DA in the back of the courtroom.

"No comment," he says while waving the reporters off, "positively no comment!"

Goldberg continues, "Your honor, during discovery, the prosecution failed to mention that there was a dog involved."

"A dog?"

"Yes your honor."

"Mr. Fisk can you explain?"

"Your honor in my deposition there was no mention of a dog. The police report has no mention of a dog at the scene," he says in aggravation as he holds his papers over his head while waving them. Fisk looks over his shoulder at Wilson; Wilson looks away.

"Mr. Goldberg, where did you get this?"

"A special source of mine found in the police records where Officer Wilson was treated for a dog bite that day. My client scuffled with Firmin, but he didn't bite Wilson; he is no dog. And to further substantiate my claim, I interviewed my client while in incarcerated and he made me aware that yes, there was a dog, Mrs. Marullo's dog. He did in fact attack Officer Wilson."

Again, Fisk glances at Wilson. "Idiot!" Fisk mumbles under his breath. Objection your honor. I fail to see the relevance."

"Mr. Goldberg I trust you know where you're going with this; overruled."

Fisk begins to mock the situation by adding, "Your honor I'm sure there were animals at the scene; some pigeons flying overhead, cats in windows, and some rats in the sewer that can testify to what they saw that day."

Laughter erupts from the court.

"You're out of order Mr. Fisk. Mr. Goldberg do you have any more witnesses?"

"Yes your honor, I have yet another expert to testify in my client's defense," he replies as he throws Fisk a look.

"Mr. Goldberg call your next witness."

"Defense calls Mr. Edward Lane."

Mr. Lane takes the witness stand.

"Mr. Lane, for the court record, would you please divulge your area of expertise?"

"Sure Mr. Goldberg, my name is Edward Lane, known to most as Ed Lane, president of the US Canine Institute. I am a certified dog trainer and have professionally trained canines for over thirty years. I presently work with several police agencies, and I specialize in all of the Schutzhund training disciplines."

"Can you expound on the Schutzhund training disciplines?"

"Certainly, it is training specifically designed for German Shepherds. This training involves the tracking and obedience work used by the AKC, and additionally, protection work that is similar to police dog work."

"Well, who would utilize this training?"

"For starters, Shepherd owners who could afford it. It is a fairly expensive training course."

Fisk becomes irritated and interrupts, "your honor I'm sure everyone appreciates Canine 101, but I fail to see the relevance."

"Before I rule, your rebuttal?"

Goldberg answers, "Sure your honor, I'm establishing character for my next witness."

"Overruled; continue Mr. Lane."

"As I was saying your honor, the purpose of this training is to demonstrate intelligence and utility; and measure mental stability, endurance, ability to scent, etc.

"Mr. Lane, how extensive is this training?"

"Well, there are three levels, the highest being the protection level."

"What does it entail?"

"The protection of its owner and attack on demand."

"So, if I sent my dog to Canine College and it got a degree, would it have completed this level?"

"It would have to," chuckling, he says, "I never really thought of it like that; yes."

"Okay Mr. Lane, thank you very much. I asked you to research the bloodline of a local dog named Bruno, owned by Mrs. Loretta Marullo. Would you please share with the court your findings?"

Lane opens his folder and reads from his notes, "Bruno, of course, AKC registered, makes it easy to trace his bloodline. And further, he was a student of mine. In fact, my records show he graduated first in his class. Excuse the pun, that would make him Magna Cum Doggie."

A roar of laughter comes from the court. Judge Jemison is visibly tickled.

"That was a good one," the judge remarks as he strikes the gavel. "Order in the court, order please."

"Bruno is from one of the purest bloodlines, traced back to the Captain Max von Stephanitz bloodline; pure personified, a highly intelligent dog."

"If a weapon was presented, how would Bruno react?"

"If said weapon was held by anyone other than the owner, that would be a signal to attack."

"Thank you Mr. Lane. That will be all."

"Would the prosecution care to cross?"

Fisk asks with attitude, "Your honor, are you serious?"

The judge dismisses Fisk's attitude and proceeds, "That'll be all. Thank you Mr. Lane. Is this mystery dog here?"

"Yes he is your honor. I'd like him to testify in actions, not words."

The court roars with laughter yet again.

"I'm probably going to be the laughingstock of this judicial section, but this young man's life hangs in the balance. I'm going to allow it."

Fisk blurts out, "Your honor, when will this circus end? First we had the feeble minded fools, the thief, then the retard, and now the zoo?"

"Your honor I object. Council has no right to pass judgment on our witnesses."

"Objection sustained. Council, please refrain from making any inappropriate comments."

Fisk seats himself abruptly, visibly aggravated.

Tiffany is cruising down the street in her convertible Beamer with her new companion. She scans the radio stations and stops when she hears the name "Kwamina Washington." Tiffany pulls over and listens intensely.

One radio speaker says, "We've been informed that closing arguments will be heard today in the Kwamina Washington case."

Another speaker adds, "Yes, I understand he is an affable young man and has the entire community rallying behind him."

"This is a high profile case and we should have a verdict today."

At this point, Tiffany turns the radio off, cups her face in her hands, and slides her hands down her face. Visibly shaken, she looks at her companion.

"Tiffany, what's going on?" he asks arrogantly.

Tiffany turns the car off.

"Tiffany what are you doing?"

"What am I doing? I still love him." Tiffany gets out of the car and walks over to the passenger side. "I don't need this. You can have it," she says as she tosses the keys to her companion. "I'm outta here!" she exclaims as she dashes toward the train station.

"With the court's cooperation your honor, I'd like to orchestrate a demonstration."

"I'll allow it."

Goldberg begins to position the two police officers to the left of the stand, and his shackled client to the far right. The court laughs. Meanwhile, Bruno is outside being prepared to enter the courtroom.

The bailiff asks, "Your honor, how do I call the next witness?"

"You dog-call and whistle," he explains as he demonstrates by whistling. "Next witness, Bruno to the stand."

Bruno's attendant says, "Okay Bruno, you go in there and you get him boy!" The attendant opens the door and Bruno enters the courtroom, somewhat confused.

Jemison calls, "Bruno, here boy."

Bruno makes his way toward the front of the courtroom. Bruno notices the two officers, stops in his tracks, shows his teeth and growls. The hair on his back stands. He cautiously advances toward them when again, he is distracted by the judge's call.

"No boy. Here, here."

Bruno then notices Kwamina and charges toward him; the court gasps, anticipating Kwamina's imminent fate. Bruno runs and leaps toward Kwamina as he braces himself to receive the onslaught of licks in the face.

"Hey boy. It's okay, it's okay".

Tail wagging, Bruno continues to lick Kwamina's face. The attendant restrains Bruno and extends his hand, while introducing himself. "Young man, I'm Frank Marullo. I'm so sorry we disrupted your life like this," he apologizes as he pats Kwamina's shoulder. "And thanks for trying to save my mom." Mr. Marullo hangs his head down and walks away with Bruno.

"Mr. Fisk, your closing argument?"

"For what it's worth, the state contests the testimony of a canine."

"Is that it?"

In exasperation, Fisk answers, "Yeah."

"To answer the state, I would have rendered this verdict prior to the dog testifying. At this time, I would like to address the court. Beyond a reasonable doubt, the scales in Lady Justice's hands are teetering toward exonerating Kwamina Washington."

Briskly standing up, Fisks says, "What?"

"Hold on, hold on. Wait a minute. I'm not finished."

Fisk relaxes and takes his seat.

"Let's start with what I just witnessed; a canine that attempted to attack two New York police officers and didn't touch the alleged suspect. The next thing was the fact that the mugging suspect left $10,000 worth of jewelry on the victim. And not to mention, he overlooked $761 on her person. I believe he was looking for her medicine. A world renowned forensics expert testifies that the woman was simply scared to death. And what scares me to death is that you have the audacity to bring to my court this spurious case. I will spearhead an investigation from City Hall to the DA's office. I am ready to render my verdict in this case," the judge announces as he looks at the bailiff.

"Gentlemen, please stand."

"Case 96-42777, State vs. Kwamina Washington. I rule in favor of the defendant. Son, you're a free man." The judge strikes his gavel and nods at the bailiff, who uncuffs Kwamina. The judge immediately diverts his attention to Dr. Stevenson.

Looking toward the heavens, Kwamina mouths the words, "Thank you." Kwamina then addresses the judge, "Thank you your honor."

Leila is sitting on the edge of the bed counting her money before servicing her client when she hears the live news report. Connie Anderson reports, "Thank you Phil. We are live here at NY Criminal Court where a not guilty verdict has just been rendered in the State vs. Kwamina Washington case."

"Connie, we expected a verdict today, but not so soon. Your take on this?" Phil asks.

"Only moments after the last defense witness, who happened to be Bruno the canine, did Judge Jemison make his ruling."

"Connie, let me remind you we're on the air."

"No kidding Phil," she says as she adjusts her earpiece. "Defense Attorney Goldberg actually found the mystery dog Bruno, who turned out to be the most effective witness. I'll have a full report at 5:00."

"Thank you Connie. Now returning back to your regular scheduled programming."

Upon hearing the not guilty verdict, Leila squeals with glee. She clutches the money to her chest and looks skyward and mouths the words, "Thank you." Tears begin to stream down her face; she sighs with a broad smile. Leila then looks at her client in disgust. Then, looking at the money, she throws it at him as if it were filthy. "I'm outta here."

Here client asks in a very demanding voice, "Hey ho, where you going?"

"To school; and I'm not your ho. In fact, I'm not anybody's ho."

As the crowd inside celebrates Kwamina's victory, Smukie, who has already worked the crowd outside, finds his conscience. Smukie identifies his victims and proceeds to return their valuables. Noticing there is no identification in the last wallet, he removes $10. Smukie mumbles to himself, "I gotta start off slow, but umma get there." In a loud voice he says, "I found a wallet on the ground. Who's wallet?"

The skinheads, while on havoc patrol, stop for a moment to hear Kwamina's not guilty verdict. "Can you believe it? That nigger got off!" The other skinheads show disgust while their leader, behind them, makes a cheerful gesture.

Kwamina hugs his attorney and thanks him as the bailiff unshackles him. Everyone rushes toward the table, rejoicing. Dr. Stevenson and the judge look on in approval and resume their conversation. Vivianna, Hakeem, and Sula make their way up to the front. The bailiff allows them to enter through the small double gates. Kwamina and Vivianna immediately embrace as Sula hugs him around his waist. Hakeem pats Kwamina on his back. Kwamina looks at Hakeem, takes his arm from around his mother's neck, and pulls Hakeem's head to his chest. Kwamina then notices Dave, and with his free hand gives him a high five. The media is held back as the family begins to walk through the courtroom. Kwamina stops when he notices Paula and Tiffany in the back. He beckons to Paula with open arms. Confused, both girls approach him while looking at each other. When they reach him, Kwamina embraces Paula and gives her a rocking hug. Tiffany visibly embarrassed, looks down. Vivianna notices Tiffany and taps Kwamina on the shoulder. Kwamina looks up at his mom as she nods is Tiffany's direction. He embraces Tiffany as she cries hysterically.

"Je suis desole. Ma punition a ete je n'ai jamais cesse de t'aimer." (I am so sorry. My punishment was, I never stopped loving you.)

"Je sais. Es-tu prete a faire parti de ceci?" (I know. Are you ready to be a part of this?)

"Oui! Yes!" Tiffany says emphatically.

Caught up in the moment of jubilant celebration, Vivianna and Dave embrace and exchange a big kiss on the lips. In shock, they both rear back, look at each other, and shake it off.

The renewed family exits the courtroom. Hakeem narrates, "Matthew 22:39, love thy neighbor as thyself and this is the result. It is so important to be kind to people; you never know if you'll need them one day. This community came together to save my brother's life. Consequently, many lives were changed for the better. Dr. Stevenson is back on staff at the university. Leila is now enrolled in creative writing classes. Tony is proud to be the great Italian he is. Smukie is holding down a job and has vowed to never steal again. Ms. Ola and Mr. Jessie are still in love. Do they know it? They'll never change. Bruno is shared by two loving families. Attorney Goldberg is practicing again and doing well. Detective Hessler and his wife now show each other affection. Mom and Uncle Dave had that weird kiss, but they are still just best friends. Mom bought the building we live in because we wanted to stay close to our friends, and she invested the rest of the money. Sula and I are doing fine. Mr. Nguyen still won't let Kwam marry Nhu, but that's okay, Kwam and Tiffany are doing great. So you see, we go through life and touch many lives. Some we experience and some we don't. All in all, if you keep God first in your life, things will always work out.

THE END

Made in the USA